1,000,000 Books

are available to read at

Forgotten Books

www.ForgottenBooks.com

Read online
Download PDF
Purchase in print

ISBN 978-1-331-42636-3
PIBN 10188527

This book is a reproduction of an important historical work. Forgotten Books uses state-of-the-art technology to digitally reconstruct the work, preserving the original format whilst repairing imperfections present in the aged copy. In rare cases, an imperfection in the original, such as a blemish or missing page, may be replicated in our edition. We do, however, repair the vast majority of imperfections successfully; any imperfections that remain are intentionally left to preserve the state of such historical works.

Forgotten Books is a registered trademark of FB &c Ltd.
Copyright © 2018 FB &c Ltd.
FB &c Ltd, Dalton House, 60 Windsor Avenue, London, SW19 2RR.
Company number 08720141. Registered in England and Wales.

For support please visit www.forgottenbooks.com

1 MONTH OF FREE READING

at

www.ForgottenBooks.com

By purchasing this book you are eligible for one month membership to ForgottenBooks.com, giving you unlimited access to our entire collection of over 1,000,000 titles via our web site and mobile apps.

To claim your free month visit: www.forgottenbooks.com/free188527

* Offer is valid for 45 days from date of purchase. Terms and conditions apply.

English
Français
Deutsche
Italiano
Español
Português

www.forgottenbooks.com

Mythology Photography **Fiction**
Fishing Christianity **Art** Cooking
Essays Buddhism Freemasonry
Medicine **Biology** Music **Ancient Egypt** Evolution Carpentry Physics
Dance Geology **Mathematics** Fitness
Shakespeare **Folklore** Yoga Marketing
Confidence Immortality Biographies
Poetry **Psychology** Witchcraft
Electronics Chemistry History **Law**
Accounting **Philosophy** Anthropology
Alchemy Drama Quantum Mechanics
Atheism Sexual Health **Ancient History**
Entrepreneurship Languages Sport
Paleontology Needlework Islam
Metaphysics Investment Archaeology
Parenting Statistics Criminology
Motivational

PART I.

HISTORICAL ESSAY

ON THE

CIVIL JURISDICTION

OF THE

ADMIRALTY.

HISTORICAL ESSAY

ON THE

CIVIL JURISDICTION

OF THE

ADMIRALTY.

THE origin and antiquity of the title, Admiral, have exercised the research and divided the opinions of many profound writers upon this subject. Such an officer is to be found in most kingdoms that border upon the sea; and it is said that Philip of France was the first who conferred that title in civilized Europe. This was in 1284 or 1286, but the same writer finds the name of this officer occurring once in the history of France, so early as the year 558. 1 And. Com. 29.— By *Du-Cange* we are informed that the Sicilians were the first, and the Genoese the next, who gave the denomination of admiral to the commanders of their naval armaments; and that it was derived from the Saracen or Arabic word *amir* or *emir*, a general name for any commanding officer. According to some writers the first admiral who is recorded in English history, was in the reign of Edward I. in 1297, and the first title of Admiral of England which was expressly conferred upon a subject, was given by patent from Richard II. in 1387, to the Earl of Arundel and Surry. But *Spelman* is of opinion that the title was first used in the reign of Henry III. because it does not occur in the laws of Oleron enacted in 1266, nor is mentioned by Bracton, who wrote about that time; and in a charter, 8 Henry, which granted the office to Richard de

Lacy, the title is not used. But in the 56th year of the same reign, the historians used the appellation, and it is likewise found in charters.

The title *Admiralis Angliæ* was not frequent until the reign of Henry IV. when the title was given to the king's brother. *Cycl. verb. Adm.*

These particulars are not without interest to many readers: but as it is neither within our purpose nor ability to investigate them fully, we leave the subject to the antiquarian and the lexicographer, and hasten to another which is more important and less enveloped in mystery.

The jurisdiction of the civil or instance court of admiralty, as it is at present understood, appears to be of a strangely anomalous kind. Mariners' wages, except where the contract is under seal or is made in an unusual manner; bottomry, in certain cases only and under many restrictions; and salvage, when the property shipwrecked is not cast ashore; appear to be the only subjects within what is now considered to be its legitimate cognizance.

By the publication of Dr. *Robinson's Reports*, we have been, however, for the first time informed, for in the common law books there is no trace of it to be found, that the court of admiralty of *England*, entertains suits for the *mere possession* of vessels though it never interferes where the *title* is in controversy. We ought also to have mentioned that the admiralty has an ancient and long recognized jurisdiction, to decide between the part owners of a ship or vessel, who differ among themselves about the policy or advantage of sending her on a particular voyage.

On considering the present state of the civil jurisdiction of the court of admiralty and tracing back its history to ancient times, we were induced to believe that those different subjects of which it now has the acknowledged cognizance, were the venerable remains of a much more extensive jurisdiction which it was long permitted to exercise, notwithstanding the restrictive statutes of 13 and 15 *Rich.* II. This opinion was confirmed by a perusal of the present work.

As the court of admiralty is constituted at present the greatest part of its proceedings in civil cases is *in rem.* Indeed it was not long ago held that it had no jurisdiction *in personam,* and that question was agitated so late as the year 1781 in the great case of *Le Caux* v. *Eden.* If, then, in the reign of *Elizabeth,* when our authour wrote, the jurisdiction of the court of admiralty had been limited as it is at present, his rules of practice would have been particularly directed to the special cases of which it had cognizance, and particularly to proceedings *in rem.* Whereas the modern subjects of admiralty jurisdiction, bottomry, salvage and mariners' wages, are not even mentioned, and only a single chapter or title (the 41st) relates to those proceedings which may properly be said to be *in rem :* for we cannot call by that name an attachment of property for the mere purpose of compelling the appearance of the defendant, on which the plaintiff does not claim any right of ownership or lien, as is the case in a suit on a bottomry bond or for seamens' wages. But it seems from the context of *Mr. Clerke's* book, that the admiralty, in his time, had cognizance of a great variety of matters and contracts which required the same modes of proceeding that are used by courts of general jurisdiction. Indeed it evidently appears that the greatest number of suits which the admiralty then entertained, were actions of debt founded upon contract, which were enforced in the first instance by the arrest of the debtor, if he was present, and by attachment of his property, in order to compel his appearance if he was absent. They entertained petitory suits, in which they decided on the title to property; as well as possessory suits, for the mere possession. No traces whatever appear of such a limited jurisdiction as the admiralty possesses at the present day. And it is remarkable that during the long reign of Queen *Elizabeth* (forty-four years) no prohibition appears to have been issued against the admiralty court, except two or three which are mentioned by Lord *Coke* in 4th *Inst.* but which we do not find elsewhere reported, and which, if his report be correct, were in violation of the agreement that will hereafter be mentioned. The admiralty jurisdiction then, as far as we are now able to trace it, extended to all cases of freight, charter parties, bottomry, mariners' wages, debts due to material men for the building and repairing of ships, and generally, to what was then considered as *maritime contracts*. It extended also to contracts made abroad, because those were to be decided according to the civil law, which was and is still the law of the admiralty. This jurisdiction was secured to that court by an agreement which was signed, in the 17th year of *Elizabeth*, by all the common law judges, in order to put an end to the disputes which their jealousy had excited and perpetually kept alive. *Vide* 4 *Inst.* 136.

But those articles, in the subsequent reigns, were not executed with good faith, any more than similar ones which were as solemnly agreed to in the eighth year of *Charles* I. *Vid. Ray.* 3. *Sea Laws* 235. The judges evaded them by subterfuges which were unworthy of the dignity of the bench, and did not observe them longer than they were constrained by the weight of royal authority. So useful, however, were they considered to be to trade and commerce, that the republican Parliament enacted them in substance by an ordinance of the 12th of *April,* 1648. *Scobell* 147. But at the Restoration, that ordinance ceased to be in force; and the common law judges began again to annoy the admiralty court with prohibitions, as they had formerly done. They did not, indeed, venture to deprive them of all their jurisdiction; they left them the cognizance of those cases of bottomry and mariners' wages which they entertain at present, but declared that they allowed it from mere indulgence and from the necessity of the thing. On the same ground a prohibition was denied in a case of mariners' wages, so early as the 8th of *James* I. *Winch.* 8. *Anonymous.*

It is certain that the court of admiralty, in its origin, had and entertained a jurisdiction co-extensive with that of the maritime courts throughout Europe. Those courts were established for the protection of maritime commerce, to which the feudal judicatures of those times were entirely inadequate. We find them in the middle ages established in all the maritime countries of christendom; in some under the name of admiralty, in others under that of consular courts. In the south of *Europe* the judges who had cognizance of commercial and maritime causes, were denominated consuls; and the celebrated code by which they were directed was thence called the consulate of the sea. *(Il Consolato del Mare.)* Those consuls were mere civil judges, unconnected with the military or feudal system; but in the north, where feudality most flourished, and where the judiciary power was considered as a necessary appendage to military grandeur, the constable, who was at the head of the land armies, and the admiral who commanded the naval forces, could not, consistently with the dignity of their stations, be without a portion of the judicial authority, while every petty baron had a court of his own. The constable therefore invested his lieutenants, as the barons did their stewards, with the power of deciding on all matters and differences which arose out of the wars; and the jurisdiction over maritime affairs naturally fell to the share of the admiral. His court was established on the model of the consular courts; and those maritime contracts which are regulated by the *Consolato del Mare* and the laws of *Oleron*, were the subject matters of their civil jurisdiction.

Of this fact there is a sufficient evidence to be found in the ancient records that are preserved in *England* in the *Black Book* of the admiralty. Among these, is an ancient statute of king *Edward* I. by which he ordained, with the consent of his barons, " that the stewards of their courts should not hold plea of any thing concerning *merchants* or *mariners*, whether it be on *charter-parties* of *vessels*, obligations or other *deeds*, even though it should be under forty shillings. Otherwise they should be proceeded against by indictment; and if found guilty by a jury of twelve men, they should be imprisoned at the discretion of the lord high admiral."*

In the reign of *Edward* III. was made the celebrated inquisition of *Queensborough*, which is to be found in *Zouch's Jurisd. of Adm. Ass. p.* 34. It contains a list of offences which the court of admiralty had then from time immemorial been authorised to inquire of and punish; and among those is that " of judges entertaining pleas of causes belonging to the admiral, and of such as in admiralty causes, sue in the courts of common law." *Zouch* 36.

---

* See the text of this statute in Master *Roughton's* articles, printed with Clerke's Praxis. p. 152, 3, 4. Edit. 1798.

This was not, we presume, directed against the king's courts, over whom we do not think that the lord high admiral ever claimed any jurisdiction or controul; but against the multitude of inferior courts with which *England* was filled at that period. The court of admiralty, indeed, claimed to be, and was then considered as one of the king's superior courts, and as such exercised the power of checking and controuling inferior jurisdictions, and particularly the baron's courts, which at that time ruled almost omnipotent within their respective precincts.

The sturdy barons could not submit to be checked in the midst of a judicial career, which was so profitable to them. For it must not be imagined that they were very ambitious of the empty honour of administering justice to their inferiors; and that, for that alone, they would have been anxious to obtain or preserve a share of the judicial authority. But a war of confiscations was then waged by the lords against their vassals. The church, on the one hand, and the nobles, on the other, by means of their judicial establishments, vied with each other in rapacity. Even down to the days of Lord *Coke*, it was a current saying, that " *Quod non capit Christus, capit fiscus.*" 3 Bulstr. 147. To secure, therefore, forfeitures, waifs, strays, heriots, deodands, and a variety of other feudal perquisites, was the real reason which induced them to keep that power in their hands. The obsequious stewards, appointed by the lords, and removable at their will, seldom failed to decide similar causes in favour of their imperious masters. Among those perquisites, not the least important to them, was that of *wrecks;* and they seldom failed to appropriate to themselves the vessels and goods which were unfortunately cast upon the *English* coast. As *wreck* was within the proper maritime jurisdiction of the lord high admiral, he interfered with them, not with a view of rescuing the shipwrecked property for the benefit of the owners, but in order to obtain it himself as a *droit* of his office. At that time several of the maritime towns enjoyed *franchises* of their own, and were exempted from the jurisdiction of feudal lords and their stewards. There the municipal authority, whose manners were softened and refined by the plastick influence of commerce and the fine arts, preserved such shipwrecked property as came within their bounds, and restored it to the lawful owner. To them the exercise of that and other parts of the admiral's jurisdiction became intolerable; and in the reign of *Richard* II. they laid their complaints before parliament.* The barons, as may be supposed, lent them a ready ear, and their remonstrances speedily procured the famous statutes of 13 *Richard* II. *cap.* 5. *and* 15 *Richard* II. *cap.* 3. by which *wreck* was, among other things, expressly excluded from the jurisdiction of the court of admiralty.

By the first of these statutes it was enacted that the admiralty should only meddle with things *done upon the sea*, as had been used in the reign of *Edward* III. and by the second that he should not have cognizance of *contracts, pleas and quarrels, and other things rising within the bodies of counties, nor of wreck*. It seems, however, that notwithstanding these statutes the court of admiralty continued to exercise its ancient jurisdiction with but little interruption from the courts of common law until the reign of *James* I. —that even in that reign and while Lord *Coke* sat on the bench, prohibitions were not frequent; that in the reign of *Charles* I. the agreement which had been made under *Elizabeth* between the courts of admiralty and common law, for the settlement of their respective jurisdictions was renewed; and it was not un-

---
* 3 *Reeves' Eng. Law.* 197.

til the reign of *Charles* II. that a serious struggle took place between the two authorities; which finally terminated in the triumph of the common law.

The contest was maintained with great ability, on the part of the civilians, by *Exton, Zouch* and *Godolphin,* all of them eminent jurists. In support of the doctrines which they defended, they displayed all the ingenuity and force of reason; but although the weight of argument was manifestly and decidedly on their side, yet the superior power and influence of the king's court of common law prevailed.

But the works of these civilians may be consulted with great advantage by those who are desirous of becoming intimately acquainted with the nature and extent of the ancient jurisdiction of the *English* court of admiralty, and the usurpations, for so they must now be called, of the courts of common law. They interpreted the statutes of *Richard* in such a manner as not to leave the court of admiralty *any civil jurisdiction* whatever. This was an interpretation which could not have been the intention of the framers of the law, who undoubtedly meant to leave them, except as to *wreck,* the same jurisdiction which they had exercised in the reign of *Edward* III. and we have seen above what that was. But the courts of common law determined that if a contract was made at sea, but to be executed on land, or made on land to be executed at sea, in either case, the common law had jurisdiction exclusive of the admiralty. What contracts then were those which remained within the jurisdiction of the latter court? Who can conceive an idea of a contract *made at sea to be performed at sea*? an instrument, for instance, made in one latitude to be executed in another? The civilians more rationally interpreted the statutes to mean, by *things and contracts done at sea,* those things and contracts, which, although the instrument by which they were proved may be made on land, yet are of a maritime nature, and are usually *performed at sea*: such as contracts of affreightment and the like; of the cognizance of which the admiralty was clearly possessed in the reign of *Edward* III.

The question, however, is now at rest in *England;* and the high court of admiralty has submitted to the restrictions which the courts of common law have imposed upon its jurisdiction. Yet in modern times, the latter have appeared to regret that those encroachments had been carried so far; and their decisions, since the time of Lord *Mansfield*, breath a spirit of much greater moderation than those of his predecessors. On several points, where it was doubtful the admiralty jurisdiction has been secured and fortified by clear and explicit adjudications; in other cases, it has been evidently enlarged; as in that of suits on bottomry contracts *under seal*. *Menetone* v. *Gibbons*, 3 *Term Rep.* 267. There it was determined that the jurisdiction of the court of admiralty does not depend on the *locality* of the contract but on the *subject matter*. This is the very principle for which the civilians have so long contended; and it only now remains to apply it with proper liberality in order to restore to the courts of admiralty, a part, at least, of that jurisdiction of which they have been deprived by the unreasonable jealousy of the courts of common law.

We should not have entered so fully into this subject, but that we think there arises out of it an important question under the constitution of the United States. By that instrument, the United States are invested with the judiciary power in all cases of *admiralty and maritime jurisdiction*. Is that jurisdiction the same which the high court of admiralty formerly possessed; or is it restricted by the statutes of *Richard* II. and the adjudication of the *English* courts founded upon them?

In the case of the *Sandwich, Pet. Adm.* 233, Judge *Winchester*, of the Maryland District, said that the statutes of 13 and 15 *Richard* II. have received in *England* a construction which must at all times prohibit their extension to this country, and he goes on to mention some instances of irreconcileable decisions under those statutes by different judges.

It was difficult for an inconsistency or a false conclusion to escape the penetrating mind of this profound lawyer, who will long be remembered among the brightest luminaries of American jurisprudence.

We are inclined to the opinion that the words *admiralty and maritime jurisdiction*, in our constitution, should be so construed as to vest in the District Courts those powers which were formerly exercised by the High Court of Admiralty. The importance of maritime commerce, the necessity of certainty and stability in its operations and the diversity of those operaations require an extensive admiralty jurisdiction.

It becomes us, however, barely to suggest this interesting question, and leave the investigation of it to those who are the proper judges and who are eminently better qualified for the task than we can pretend to be.

For particular information on the subject of the *present* jurisdiction of the civil or instance court of admiralty in *England* and of the laws and forms by which its proceedings are governed, the reader is referred to *Brown's Civil and Admiralty Law*, in which the subject is treated in a luminous, methodical, and comprehensive manner.

There are but a few decisions of our own courts which make any change on the subject of jurisdiction. The most important are, 1 Dalk 49. 3 Dall. 297. 4 Cranch 24, 443, 447, 452.

Our admiralty is yet in its infancy, and we must wait for the slow hand of time to unfold the extent of its powers. The forms of proceeding are equally unsettled and various. We shall therefore, by the advice of a judicious friend, subjoin a collection of approved precedents.

To gratify the curiosity of those who wish to pursue the investigation of the subject of which we have taken a cursory view in this introduction, we shall add the following documents :

1. The ordinance of *Hastings*, made by King *Edward* I. on the subject of admiralty jurisdiction : extracted from the Black Book of the Admiralty :

2. The heads of the articles of the Inquisition of *Queensborough*, taken in the 49th year of *Edward* III. by eighteen expert seamen ;[*] before the Admirals of the North and West and the Lord Warden of the Cinque Ports.

3. The *Articuli Admiralitatis*, or remonstrance of the Court of Admiralty to King *James* I. complaining of the violation of the articles agreed upon and signed by all the common law judges in the 17th year of *Elizabeth*, with Lord *Coke's* evasive answer.

---

[*] Probably a Grand Jury of Mariners.

COURT OF ADMIRALTY.

4. The Resolution signed by all the common law judges in the 8th year of King *Charles* I. on the subject of admiralty jurisdiction and afterwards disavowed.

5. The Ordinance made by the Republican Parliament of *England*, in 1648, on the subject of admiralty jurisdiction.

A.

Ordinance of Hastings on the subject of Admiralty Jurisdiction.

Extract from the Black Book of the Admiralty, C.—Art. 20.

(TRANSLATION.)

It was ordained at *Hastings* by King *Edward* I. and his Lords, that whereas divers Lords had various franchises of trying pleas in sea-ports; their Stewards or Bailiffs should not hold any plea, if it concerned merchants or mariners, whether by *Deed, Charter-party* of vessels, *Obligations* or other *Deeds;* even though the sum should not exceed 20s. or 40s. and that if any one act to the contrary, and should thereon be indicted, and be thereof convicted, judgment should be given against him as is said above.

Vide *Clerke's Praxis, Lond. Edit.* 1743. page 153.

B.

Heads of the Articles of the Inquisition taken at Quinborow in the year 1376, *in the* 49th *of King Edward the Third, by eighteen expert seamen, before William Nevil, Admiral of the North, Philip Courteney, Ad-*

miral *of the West, and the Lord Latimer, Warden of the Cinque Ports.*

I. OFFENCES AGAINST THE KING AND KINGDOM.

1. Of such as did furnish the enemy with victuals and ammunition, and of such as did traffic with the enemies without special licence.

2. Of Traytors goods detained in ships and concealed from the King.

3. Of Pirates, their receivers, maintainers and consorters.

4. Of murthers, manslaughters, maimes and petty felonies committed in ships.

5. Of ships arrested for king's service; breaking the arrest; and of sergeants of the admiralty, who for money discharge ships arrested for the king's service; and of mariners who having taken pay, run away from the king's service.

II. OFFENCES AGAINST THE PUBLIC GOOD OF THE KINGDOM.

1. Of ships transporting gold and silver.

2. Of carrying corn over sea without special licence.

3. Of such as turn away merchandizes or victuals from the king's ports.

4. Of forestallers, regrators, and of such as use false measures, balances, weights, within the jurisdiction of the admiralty.

5. Of such as make spoil of wrecks, so that the owners, coming within a year and a day cannot have their goods.

6. Of such as claim wrecks, having neither charter nor prescription.

COURT OF ADMIRALTY.

7. Of wears riddles, blindstakes, water mills, &c. whereby ships and men have been lost or endangered.

8. Of removing anchors, and cutting of buoy-ropes.

9. Of such as take salmons at unreasonable times.

10. Of such as spoil the breed of oisters or drag for oisters and muscles at unreasonable times.

11. Of such as fish with unlawful nets.

12. Of taking royal fishes, viz. whales, sturgeons, purpoises, &c. and detaining one half from the king.

III. OFFENCES AGAINST THE ADMIRAL, THE NAVY, AND DISCIPLINE OF THE SEA.

1. Of judges entertaining pleas of causes belonging to the admiral, and of such as in admiralty causes sue in the courts of common law, and of such as hinder the execution of the admiral's process.

2. Of masters and mariners contemptuous to the admiral.

3. Of the admiral's shares of waifs or derelicts, and of deodands belonging to the admiral.

4. Of *Flotson, Jetson,* and *Lagon,* belonging to the admiral.

5. Of such as freight strangers' bottoms, where ships of the land may be had at reasonable rates.

6. Of ship-wrights taking excessive wages.

7. Of masters and mariners taking excessive wages.

8. Of pilots, by whose ignorance ships have miscarried.

9. Of mariners forsaking their ships.

10. Of mariners rebellious and disobedient to their masters.

Vide Zouch's *Jurisd. of the Adm. asserted, page* 34.

C.

Articuli Admiralitatis.

The complaint of the Lord Admiral of England to the King's Most Excellent Majesty, against the Judges of the Realm, concerning prohibitions granted to the Court of the Admiralty 11 *die Febr. ultimo die Termini Hilarii, Anno* 8. *Jac Regis.* The effect of which complaint was after, by his Majesty's commandment, set down in Articles by Doctor Dun, Judge of the Admiralty, which are as followeth.

Certain grievances whereof the Lord Admiral and his officers of the Admiralty do especially complain, and desire redress.

1. That whereas the conusance of all contracts and other things done upon the sea belongeth to the Admiral jurisdiction, the same are made triable at the Common Law, by supposing the same to have been done in Cheapsides, and such places.

2. When actions are brought in the Admiralty upon bargains and contracts made beyond the seas, wherein the Common Law cannot administer justice, yet in these cases prohibitions are awarded against the Admiral Court.

2. Whereas time out of mind the Admiral Court hath used to take stipulations for appearance and performance of the acts and judgments of the same court: It is now affirmed by the judges of the Common Law the Admiral Court is no court of record, and therefore not able to take such stipulations: And hereupon prohibitions are granted to the utter overthrow of that jurisdiction.

4. That charter-parties, made only to be performed upon the seas are daily withdrawn from that court by prohibitions.

5. That the clause of *non obstante statuto*, which hath foundation in his Majesty's prerogative, and is current in all other grants, yet in the Lord Admiral's Patent is said to be of no force to warrant the determination of the causes committed to him in his Lordship's patent, and so rejected by the Judges of the Common Law.

5. To the end that the Admiral jurisdiction may receive all manner of impeachment and interruption, the rivers beneath the first bridge where it ebbeth and floweth, and the ports and creeks, are by the judges of the Common Law affirmed to be no part of the seas, nor within the Admiral jurisdiction: And whereupon prohibitions are usually awarded upon actions depending in that court, for contracts and other things done in those places; notwithstanding that by use and practice, time out of mind, the admiral court have had jurisdiction within such ports, creeks, and rivers.

7. That the agreement made Anno Domini 1575, between the Judges of the King's Bench, and the Court of Admiralty for the more quiet and certain execution of Admiral Jurisdiction, is not observed as it ought to be.

8. Many other grievances there are, which by discussing of these former will easily appear worthy also of reformation.

The following is the answer of the Common Law Judges, drawn up by Sir Edward Coke, to the 7th of the above articles of complaint.

ANSWER: The supposed agreement mentioned in this article hath not as yet been delivered unto us, but having heard the same read over before his Majesty, (out of a paper not subscribed with the hand of any Judge) we answer, that for so much thereof as differeth from these answers, it is against the laws and statutes of the realm : and *therefore* the Judges of the King's Bench never assented thereunto, as is pretended, neither doth the phrase thereof agree with the terms of the law of the realm.

Vide 4th Inst. 134.

D.

Resolution upon the Cases of Admiral Jurisdiction.

Whitehall, 18th February. Present, the King's Most Excellent Majesty.

Lord Keeper,	Earl of Morton,
Lord Abp. of York,	Lord V. Wimbleton,
Lord Treasurer,	Lord V. Wentworth,
Lord Privy Seal,	Lord V. Falkland,
Earl Marshal,	Lord Bishop of London,
Lord Chamberlain,	Lord Cottington,
Earl of Dorset,	Lord Newburgh,
Carlisle,	Mr. Treasurer,
Holland,	Mr. Comptroller,
Denbigh,	Mr. Vice Chamberlain,
Lord Chancellor of Scotland.	Mr. Secretary *Coke*,
	Mr Secretary Windebauk.

This day the King being present in Council, the Articles and propositions following for the accommodating and settling the difference concerning Prohibitions, arising between his Majesty's Courts at Westminster, and his Court of Admiralty, were fully debated and resolved by the Board : and were then likewise upon reading the same, as well before the Judges of his Majesty's said Courts at Westminster, as before the Judge of his said Court of Admiralty, and his Attorney General, agreed unto, and subscribed by them all in his Majesty's presence, *viz :*

1. If suit should be commenced in the Court of Admiralty upon contracts made or other things personal done beyond the seas or upon the sea, no prohibition is to be awarded.

2. If suit be before the admiral for freight or mariner wages, or for breach of charter-parties, for wages to be made beyond the seas; though the charter-party happen to be made within the realm; so as the penalty be not demanded, a prohibition is not to be granted. But if the suit be for the penalty, or if the question be made, whether the charter-party be made or not; or whether the plaintiff did release, or otherwise discharge the same within the realm; this is to be tried in the King's Courts, and not in the Admiralty.

3. If suit be in the Court of Admiralty, for building, amending, saving or necessary victualling of a ship, against the ship itself, and not against any party by name, but such as for his interest makes himself a party; no prohibition is to be granted, though this be done within the realm.

4. Altho' of some causes arising upon the Thames beneath the Bridge, and divers other rivers beneath the first Bridge, the King's Courts have cognizance; yet the Admiralty hath also jurisdiction there, in the point specially mentioned in the statute of *Decimo quinto Richardi Secundi*, and also by exposition and equity thereof, he may enquire of and redress all annoyances, and obstructions in those rivers, that are any impediment to navigation or passage to or from the sea; and no prohibition is to be granted in such cases.

5. If any be imprisoned, and, upon habeas corpus brought, it be certified, that any of these be the cause of his imprisonment, the party shall be remanded.

Subscribed 4th February, 1632, by all the Judges of both benches.—Vide *Cro. Car.* 296. *Ed. Lond.* 1657. By Sir Harbottle Grimstone.

Sir George Cooke was one of the judges who subscribed these resolutions, and he inserted them in his reports, no doubt considering them as law, yet they were afterwards disavowed and said to have been renounced by several of the Judges. Raym. 3.

" These resolutions," says *Brown,* 2 Civ. and Adm. L. 79, " are inserted in the *early* editions of Coke's " Reports ; but left out in the later, seemingly *ex in-* " *dustriá.*" And page 78 he says, " To these resolu- " tions the objection cannot be made, which is urged " by my Lord Coke (4 Inst. 136) to the agreement of " 1575, that though it was read over in his Majesty's " presence, and in the hearing of the Judges, yet it " was never assented to."

E.

Extract from Scobell's Collection of the Acts and Ordinances of the Republican Government of England. Anno 1648—*page* 147.

CHAPTER 112.

The Jurisdiction of the Court of Admiralty settled.

The Lords and Commons assembled in Parliament, finding many inconveniences daily to arise, in relation both to the trade of this Kingdom, and the Commerce with foreign parts, through the uncertainty of jurisdiction in the trial of maritime causes, do ordain and be it ordained by the authority of Parliament, That the Court of Admiralty shall have cognizance and jurisdiction against the ship or vessel, with the tackle, apparel and furniture thereof; in all causes which concern the repairing, victualling and furnishing provisions for the setting of such ships or vessels to sea ; and in all cases of bottomry, and likewise in contracts made beyond the seas concerning shipping or navigation or damages happening thereon, or arising at sea in any voyage; and likewise in all cases of charter parties or contracts for freight, bills of lading, mariners' wages, or damages in goods laden on board ships, or other damages done by one ship or vessel to another, or by anchors, or want of laying of buoys, except always that the said Court of Admiralty shall not hold pleas or admit actions upon any bills of exchange or accounts betwixt merchant and merchant or their factors.

And be it ordained, That in all and every the matters aforesaid, the said Admiralty Court shall and may proceed and take recognizances in due form, and hear, examine, and finally end, decree, sentence and determine the same according to the laws and customs of the sea, and put the same decrees and sentences in execution without any let, trouble or impeachment whatsoever, any law, statute or usage to the contrary heretofore made in any wise notwithstanding; saving always and reserving to all and every person and persons, that shall find or think themselves aggrieved by any sentence definitive, or decree having the force of a definitive sentence, or importing a damage not to be repaired by the definitive sentence given or interposed in the Court of Admiralty, in all or any of the cases aforesaid, their right of appeal in such form as hath heretofore been used from such decrees or sentences in the said Court of Admiralty.

Provided always, and be it further ordained by the authority aforesaid, that from henceforth there shall be three judges always appointed of the said court, to be nominated from time to time by both houses of Parliament or such as they shall appoint; and that every of the judges of the said court for the time being, that shall be present at the giving of any definitive sentence in the said Court, shall at the same time, or before such sentence given openly in Court, deliver his reasons in law of such his sentence, or of his opinion concerning the same; and shall also openly in Court give answers and solutions (as far as he may) to such laws, customs or other matter as shall have been brought or alleged in Court, on that part against whom such sentence or opinion shall be given or dclared respectively.

Provided also, That this Ordinance shall continue for three years and no longer.

Passed, the 12th April 1648.

Made perpetual by Ordinances of 2nd April, 1641. C. 3.—1654. C. 21. and 1645. C. 10.

Expired at the Restoration, anno 1660.

PART II.

THE PRACTICE

OF THE

HIGH COURT OF ADMIRALTY,

BY FRANCIS CLERKE.

TRANSLATED FROM THE LAST EDITION,

WITH NOTES AND ADDITIONS.

TRANSLATION

Of the Preface to the Fifth Edition.

Courteous Reader,

Accept a brief account of this new edition of the Praxis, with which I wish thee to be acquainted.— Francis Clerke was a man of great skill and industry, who, not without credit, held the office of a Proctor in the Court of Arches, during the reign of Elizabeth. Besides this Book on the Practice of the Court of Admiralty, he composed another on that of the Ecclesiastical Court, which he originally intended for his own use. And having no view of exposing them to the publick eye, he hath paid less attention to the digesting and explanation of the principles, upon which these rules are founded.

After his decease, these manuscripts were anxiously sought, and eagerly copied by divers Advocates and Proctors: because, as yet there were no books extant on the subjects whereof they treat. And thus, at length, by a certain evil fate, they chanced to fall into the hands of mercenary men and *half scholars*, who, being exceedingly covetous of a dishonest gain, and having, moreover, no regard to the name or reputation of the author, now dead, did not blush to publish these books, which were only intended for private use, disgraced by manifold omissions and typographical errours.

The work in which the Practice of the Ecclesiastical Court is treated of, hath indeed, lately been diligently corrected and happily reduced to method, by Master *Oughton*, a man well skilled in such matters. But this, its father being no more, hath hitherto lain so neglected and exposed, and withal so transformed throughout, that it could scarcely be recognized by the authour himself, if he were to rise from his grave. And it is likewise so mutilated and imperfect, that not a single chapter, verily, scarce a paragraph in the former editions, can be consulted with safety, much less understood. But before it was published we know, certainly, that it was held in such high estimation by learned men and all professors of the Law, that they copied it with their own hands.

And this is the reason that the edition which we now present to thee, friendly reader, is produced thus correct. For it hath been collated with two manuscripts, one of which is in the hand-writing of Dr. LAW, and the other of ROBERT WISEMAN, L. L. D. and Knight,* both of whom were distinguished ornaments of their Country and the Civil Law. The former was not long since, a Fellow of the Holy Trinity College, Cambridge, and the latter was Keeper of the same, and a liberal benefactor to it. These copies became the property of the College, by the donation of that most accomplished man NATHANIEL LLOYD, L. L. D. and Knight, who not long since, was the most worthy Keeper of the College, and lived and died its distinguished benefactor.

The Notes distinguished by this mark [" "] were communicated to me by a most learned friend from a manuscript in his possession, which he supposeth to have been written by a certain *Tobias Swinburne*, a not unworthy relative of the writer on Wills of the same name.

[* Sir Robert Wiseman, a Civilian and Dean of the Arches, married the sister of Francis North, Baron of Guilford, Lord Keeper of the Great Seal in the reigns of Charles II. and James II. With this eminent Judge he "observed a more than brotherly correspondence until his death." Life of Lord Guilford, p. 306. Of Dr. Eden, I have not found any mention.]

PRACTICE

OF THE

HIGH COURT OF ADMIRALTY.

Tit. 1. *Of the manner of instituting or commencing an action in the High Court of Admiralty of England; and of the form of the original warrant or mandate which is to be impetrated in Maritime Causes.*

IF any person have cause to maintain an action of a civil or maritime nature, it is necessary for him in the first place to procure a warrant or mandate from the Judge,[1] to these effects respectively, to wit: to arrest and hold the defendant, and to detain him in sufficient custody until he has legally appeared,[*] or that he shall have produced his body on a certain day, viz. on the third, fourth, fifth, sixth, seventh, eighth or tenth day next ensuing that of his arrest, according to the distance of the defendant's place of residence, provided it be a return day; otherwise on the next return-day following, at the Court-

---

[1] In this country it is to be procured from the Clerk of the Court.—*Tr.*]

[*] What shall be deemed a legal appearance. Vid. Tit. 5. *seq.*

House where justice is administered, or where it is usually administered, in the borough of Southwark, near the London bridge, before the honourable the Lord High Admiral of England, or his Lieutenant,[2] the President or Judge of the Supreme Court of Admiralty, to answer unto N. merchant of London, in a certain civil or maritime cause, as to justice shall seem meet and proper.

[2 The title of *locum tenens Regis super mare*, the king's lieutenant general of the sea, mentioned in the reign of Rich. II. was superior to that of *admiral* of England. Before the appellation of *admiral* was introduced, the title of *custos maris* was in use.

In some ancient records the Lord High Admiral is called *capitanus maritimarum*. There has been no such office for some years, but his duties have been exercised by *Lords* commissioners of the Admiralty, who possess the same jurisdiction.—2. W. & M.—c. 2.

The modern style of the Judge of the High Court of Admiralty in England, is, LIEUTENANT of the HIGH COURT of ADMIRALTY of ENGLAND *and in the same court official principal and commissary general and special, and President and Judge thereof.* Formal. Instrument. by Sir James Marriott, 245.

He may delegate his powers to an inferior Judge called Surrogate *(Judex subrogatus*, substituted Judge) and that deputy may hear causes and even to proceed to final judgment: *ib.* 246. There are similar Surrogates or deputy Judges in the Ecclesiastical Courts. Hence in some of the United States, in New-York, particularly, the name of *Surrogate* has been given to the officer who has cognizance of the probate of wills and granting letters of administration, although that officer does not exercise his functions by deputation. In other States as in Pennsylvania and Maryland, he is called Register, from the denomination which is given in England to the Clerks of Ecclesiastical Courts. Both these appellations appear to me to be incorrect. That of *Judge* of *Probate*, which is used in Massachusetts, is much more applicable and conveys a more just idea of the office, which it is meant to designate.—*Tr.*]

Additions to Title 1.

A CITATION or *in jus vocatio*, is a judicial act whereby the defendant by authority of the Judge, (the plaintiff requesting it) is commanded to appear in order to enter into suit at a certain day, in a place where justice is administered.

The citation ought to contain,

1. The name of the Judge and his commission, if he be delegated; if an ordinary Judge, with the style of the Court of which he is Judge.
2. The name of him who is to be cited.
3. An appointed day and place where he must appear; which day ought either to be expressed particularly to be such a day of the week or month, &c. or else only the next Court day (or longer) from the date of the citation, in which the Judge sits to administer justice: the time of appearance ought to be more or less, according to the distance of the place where they live.
4. The cause for which the suit is to be commenced.
5. The name of the party at whose instance the citation is obtained.

These words may also be added, viz. If the said day be a court-day, or otherwise, the next court-day following, in which the Judge happens to sit to administer justice. The reason of this is, lest that day of the month so particularized in the citation should happen to be a holy-day, which is no day for administering justice.

The days called in the law, *dies juridici* are such as are only proper and suitable, and set apart in the law for judicial acts; in which respect they are termed opposites to holy-days; these being exempt from all judicial acts, and rendering them null and void, if attempted to be executed on such days. *Consetio's Practice of Spiritual and Ecclesiastical Courts, London* 1708. p. 3.

It is also usual for citations to be issued forth against the defendant to appear the third, fourth, sixth, or other day next following the citation, wherein the Judge happens to sit judicially to try causes (no day of the month being named) and this is called *dies incertus*, only in respect of the time when he must appear; the other necessaries and constitutive parts of the citations (*scil.*) *de quo et an et cui extiturus sit*, being complete. In which case, it is necessary that the defendant repair immediately to the place where the Court is to be kept, and inform himself certainly what day of the week or month is the day intended for his appearance, lest his adversary get the advantage by his not appearing. *ib.*

By the act of Congress, July 20, 1789, sec. 2. Mariners are entitled to demand one third part of the wages which shall be due at every port where the vessel shall unlade and deliver her cargo before the voyage be ended, unless the contrary be expressly stipulated in the contract. If the wages be not paid within ten days after the termination of the voyage and the discharge of the cargo or ballast, or if there be any dispute between the seamen and the master respecting the wages, the Judge of the district where the vessel may be, may summon the master before him to show cause why process should not issue against the vessel, according to the course of Admiralty Courts, to answer for the wages. If his residence be more than three miles from the place or if he be absent from his place of residence a summons may be obtained from any Judge or Justice of the peace. Upon the master's neglect to appear, or if he appear and do not show that the wages are paid, or otherwise satisfied or forfeited, the Judge or Justice certifies to the clerk of the District Court that there is sufficient cause of complaint whereon to found Admiralty-process. The clerk then issues process against the ship and the suit is proceeded on and final judgment given according to the usual course of Admiralty Courts.

In such suits, all the seamen, having cause of complaint of the like kind against the same ship are joined as complainants; but it has been decided by Judge Houston, of Maryland District, that such consolidation of claims does not prevent the seamen from being sworn as witnesses. The act further protects them, by making it incumbent on the master to produce the contract and logbook if required, to ascertain any matter in dispute, or the complainants are permitted to state the contents thereof, and the *onus probandi* the contrary lies upon the master. The District Courts have not exclusive cognizance of disputes concerning wages, but seamen may maintain any action at common law for the recovery of them. Seamen are entitled to immediate process without the previous summons, out of any Court possessing Admiralty jurisdiction, wherever the ship may be found, in case she shall have left the port of delivery where her voyage ended, or in case she shall be about to proceed to sea before the expiration of the ten days, ensuing the delivery of her cargo or ballast. 1. Laws U. S. 140.

Such are the statutory provisions respecting suits for mariners' wages. In the case of Edwards *vs.* the ship Susan, *Pennsylvania District*, the question arose, at what time a mariner, at the last port of delivery, is entitled to receive or sue for his wages? Judge Peters, in his decision, said, that it had always appeared to him unwarrantable to contend that the ten days should run from the time of the discharge of the cargo. He thought that the end of the voyage was, clearly the period when the wages, according to the contract were due. The discharge of the cargo or ballast, is coupled with the end of the voyage in the law, not as part of the contract, or to fix the time, from which the ten days are to be computed; but because it is a necessary step to enable the merchant to demand his freight: and the wages ought not to be paid, until this is recoverable; it being the fund out of which the wages are payable. He considered himself authorised to inquire into the circumstances peculiar to each case, and in the exercise of this discretion, he had allowed at the least, ten days from the end of the voyage, and at the most, fifteen working days to unlade. By the *end of the voyage*, he understood, the day on which the vessel was made fast to the wharf and ready to discharge. Pet. Adm. Dec. 165.

I will barely add, that in all other cases where the District Court exercises an Admiralty jurisdiction, the course of proceeding is, to file a libel, in which the causes of complaint are alleged. Upon the receipt of the libel a monition and attachment are issued of course, by the Clerk and served by the Marshal.]

TIT. 2. *Of the direction of the Warrant.*

THE Warrant is issued in the name of the Lord High Admiral of England,[3] and it must be directed to all and singular the Justices, Constables, Mayors, Bailiffs, and other officers of our Lord the King, particularly to D. Marshal of the High Court of Admiralty of England. It is usual for the Registrar[4] of the Court to issue this Warrant without a special decree for the purpose, in the same manner that primary or common citations are issued in the Ecclesiastical Courts.

[3 Such was the practice in England at the time when our authour wrote, but at present it appears to be different. All processes and even forms of decrees that are recorded in Sir James Marriott's Formulary of authentick writs, run in the name of the King. *Vid. Form. Inst. passim.*

In the United States Courts, every process in the District, as well as in the Circuit Courts, is in the name of The United States.—*Tr.*]

[4 In *Dyer* 152 *b.* there is a prescription, for the Lord High Admiral to grant the Office of Registrar of the Admiralty for life. In this country the Clerks of the District Courts of the United States are appointed by the Courts respectively in which they act, and hold their Offices at will.—*Tr.*]

Tit. 3. *Of the manner of executing the Warrant.*

When you have obtained such a Warrant as has been described, it is to be delivered to the Marshal of the Court* (*i. e.* to a certain officer who is specially appointed for this particular purpose) if the person who is to be arrested resides or is to be found within the City of London, the suburbs or adjacent places. Otherwise to some Mayor, Bailiff, Constable, or any Officer or Assistant, in whatever City, Village or Town, where the person lives, who is to be arrested. And the person to whom it is delivered, by virtue of the Warrant shall arrest the defendant, and shall notify to him the cause of the arrest, at the same time exhibiting the Warrant to him. He shall then lodge him in gaol or detain him in safe custody, unless he shall give sufficient security for his legal appearance on the day and at the place mentioned in the Warrant, and shall answer the plaintiff in the action which has been instituted. Which being done he shall be released from the arrest.

Additions to Title 3.

[If the party cited request a copy of this citation, the officer ought to give him a copy, and

---

* If the process is to be served within twenty miles from the City of London, it is to be given to the Marshal, but if at a greater distance, it is committed to the party who applies for it.

receive only six pence for that copy, if it be an ordinary or usual citation.—*Cons.*]

Tit. 4. *Of the* caution or bail to be given by the person who is arrested, for his legal appearance.*

In the margin or at the foot of the Warrant to which the seal of the Lord High Admiral is affixed, the sum for which the action was brought is marked in these words: *action for £500.* The security which is taken ought therefore to be to the amount of the sum thus specified † for the legal appearance of the party, for the purposes before mentioned, to wit: to answer the plaintiff in the civil and maritime cause. The Officer who executes the Warrant should therefore be cautious that his security be good and sufficient before he release the defendant, as he himself is liable to an action, if the defendant should not appear.‡ The security being taken, the War-

---

* It is not proper to accept as bail to abide the sentence, (fidejussor judicio sisto) a person who has no property within the territory. *Scaccia de appell. quæs.* 15. nu. 139.

† This security should be taken in the name of the Lord High Admiral. [In the District Courts of the United States it is taken in the name of the Marshal. *Tr.*]

‡ Vid. l. 1. Digest. Si quis in jus vocat. et Bald. et Castr. et Dd. ibid. vid. Joseph. Ludov. Decis. Lucens. 33. who says that a Notary receiving improper security becomes liable, except in three cases:

1st. When he does it by order of the Judge.

2nd. When the principal is solvent, *i. e.* possesses as much property as the amount of the bond.

rant and the bond are to be transmitted before the day of appearance, to the Judge, Registrar, Plaintiff, or to his Proctor, together with the name and surname of the person who executed the process, and the time and place of executing it, in order that an authentick certificate of the execution may be made out and exhibited.

ADDITIONS TO TITLE 4.

[Securities, or cautions, as they are termed by Civilians, are of three sorts :
1. *Judicatum Solvi;* by which the party is bound absolutely to pay such sum as may be adjudged by the Court.
2. *De Judicio Sisti;* by which he was bound to appear from time to time during the pendency of the cause, to abide the sentence and also to pay a tenth part of the sum in dispute if he should be defeated.
3. *De Ratio;*[b] by which he engaged to ratify and confirm the acts of his Proctor.

With respect to the manner in which these cautions were taken, they were,
1. *Cautio fidejussoria;* by sureties.

3d. When he receives it in the presence of the party, who does not protest against it.

The Judges are not liable, see §. last Inst. de Satisdat. tuto. vid. Vincen. de Franch. decis. 480. n. 3. Farinac. part 1st. prax. crimin. quest. 33.

[b *De Ratio* is not Latin. I find that Brown 2 Civ. & Adm. Law 356. has it *ratio;* but it is clearly a mistake. The true word is *Rato;* it is so in all the best texts.—*Tr.*]

2. *Pignoratitia;* by deposit.
3. *Juratoria;* by oath.'
4. *Nudi Promissoria;* by bare promise.—
Cons.

The securities in the Admiralty, though in the nature of recognizance, do not authorize the Courtto proceed against lands.—*Tr.*]

TIT. 5. *What shall constitute a legal appearance.*

IF the party arrested, or his lawful Proctor shall personally appear, at the return-day by virtue of the Warrant, together with new security (for that which was taken at the time of his arrest, was only bound for the appearance of the person arrested, as in the preceding title) bound to the effects respectively enumerated in Tit. 12, *(of the security given by the defendant)* he has completed a legal security, otherwise not. But if the party himself appear in person, with security to the effect of the aforesaid obligation, he is to be committed to prison by the Judge, until the termination of the suit, unless in the interim he put in bail.* Nevertheless the Judge may, upon proper causes, admit the party to his juratory caution,† viz: the oath of the party to the same effects for which bail should have been

---

[' This security is given when the party is too poor to find actual bail. It is in the discretion of the Judge. *Tr.*]

* In patriâ seu territorio vocato in judicium succurritur, obcausas sonticas absentia; (non solum morbum, sed tempestatem, quæ impedit navigationem et iter) quæ probanda. Locc. 3. c. II. §. 4. 5.

† Vid. Capell. Tholoss. quæs. 138. n. 2.

given; particularly if it should appear to him that the party is so poor that he is unable to find security. And if the party shall bring the aforesaid new security, or shall be committed for want of them, or if the Judge shall admit the juratory caution, the former security for his appearance shall be discharged, the bail-bond is to be delivered up, and the party arrested is to be released.

TIT. 6. *The execution of the Warrant.*

IF the Warrant have been executed by the Marshal, or by any of the Deputy Marshals of the Court, then the same Officer is accustomed to make his corporal oath, that at such a day and in such a place, he arrested the defendant according to the tenor of the Warrant. But if the Warrant was executed without the City of London, or the suburbs, by a Mayor or any of the Officers specified above in Tit. 2. the Proctor of the plaintiff shall procure a certificate of the execution of the Warrant at length, specifying the day and place of its execution: and he should have it sealed with an authentick seal, in order that full credit may be given to it.

TIT. 7. *Of the Warrant of Attorney or Proxy.*[8]

THE Warrant of Attorney or Proxy in civil and maritime causes, is made in the same form

---

[8 The Civil Law distinguishes, as we do, between a Letter and a Warrant of Attorney. The former is called a procuration, proxy, procuracy, or procuratory, with the Proxy or Procuratory *ad lites*, in Ecclesiastical causes; and it contains all those clauses and powers general and particular which are usually contained in them, with these exceptions: that in the commencement of the proxy to conduct an Ecclesiastical suit, power is given to the Proctor *in omnibus causis* negotiis, litibus et *querelis;* but in civil causes, after the words *litibus et querelis*, the words *civilibus et maritimis* are added. Proxies of this kind, in order to be authentick should be sealed with an authentick seal, in the same manner that such papers are in the Ecclesiastical Courts.* In the Proxies which are filed in Ecclesiastical causes, power is likewise given to petition for the benefit of absolution or liberation from whatever decrees of excommunication, or of interdiction, suffered or to be suffered by law or man, whether simply or by bond. But in Proxies in civil causes, that clause is to be omitted and another is to be inserted, by which power is given to the Proctor to give and introduce, *Ligios, cautiones et Fidejussores*, and also to demand and receive them from the opposite party.

---

ad negotia, and the former *ad lites;* that is to say, the one is an authority given to an Attorney in fact, and is a matter extra-judicial, or, *in pays*, and the latter is an authority given to an Attorney at Law, to manage or prosecute one or more suits, or all suits, and is a matter of record, because it is always filed among the exhibits of the cause, and sometimes is executed before and attested by the Clerk or Register of the Court. In the last case, it is said to be made *apud acta*, in the acts of Court.—*Tr.*]

* Cler. Praxis per Oughtonum, Tit. 48.

Additions to Title 5.

[A Proctor is constituted either by proxy or *apud acta curiæ*, or before a Notary Publick and witnesses.

A Proxy, (which *Wesembecy* ranks in the number of extra-judicial constitutions, as also the other before a Notary Publick) is a power or mandate given to the Proctor by his client to appear for him, and to do all things for him, which he might possibly do, if he were personally there himself; with power to substitute another in his stead, so often as he shall be absent upon urgent occasions. And that it may be valid and authentick it ought to contain the name of the party constituting and the name of the Proctor constituted; also against whom, in what cause, before what Judge, and to what acts he is constituted, (viz.) to act, offer, or receive a libel; to except, contest suit, produce witnesses, hear sentence, &c. in which respect these mandates or proxies may be said to be either general (giving full power to prosecute the whole cause while it is in controversy) or special (which gives power only to do or perform some particular act, &c.) and this mandate, that it may be authentick, must be sealed in the same form as authentick certificates (before mentioned) are sealed; of which, see *Lindwood*, Constitutioni *Othoboni, C. d. officio procuratorum*. These mandates ought likewise to make mention, that they are ready to confirm whatsoever their said Proctor shall do in the premises.

Another sort of extra-judicial Constitution is that which is made before a Notary Publick, who draws up a publick instrument thereupon, and exhibits it in Court; and likewise a Proctor is constituted before two or more witnesses, who give their testimony concerning this Constitution of the Proctor. A Proctor is only then said to be constituted judicially, when the party constituting is present in Court, and makes choice of his Proctor before the Judge, and confirms his person, and promises to ratify whatsoever his said Proctor shall act or do (which election he desires may be put into the Court act) or when he, or some one in his name, offers to the Judge a letter, or other writing, which makes appear whom he makes choice of for a Proctor; the contents of which is to be inserted in the acts of the Court. Mr. *Clerke* seems to reckon a constitution before a Notary Publick to be a judicial constituting of a Proctor, but the mistake will easily appear by Wesembecy ff. T. *de Procurator.*' Cons. Prac. 30.]

TIT. 8. *Of constituting a Proctor* apud acta, *or extra-judicially before a Notary.*

THE plaintiff or defendant if he is present in Court at the commencement of the suit, gene-

---

[* As to the form and manner of constituting a Proctor, see further *Wesemb. ff. de procur.* numb. 5, 6. Myns. 46. 1. *Maranta. in Specul. par.* 4. *dist.* 1. *n.* 35. in *Prac.* and Spec. in *tit. de procur. Sect. rationæ form.* numb. 13. 19. and n. 4. *Cuja. obs.* l. 7. c. 26. in prac. 12. n. 2.—*Tr.*]

rally executes a proxy for the cause in a judicial manner, with all the clauses which are usually inserted in proxies and according to the style of the Court and the precedent written by the Register; by which he stipulates to ratify all the acts and things done by his Proctor. And the Register shall receive a Warrant of Attorney and stipulation of this kind, and shall take the person so constituting and stipulating by the right hand[10] in token thereof. And this sort of appointment may be done before the Register in his own house, in the presence of witnesses.— This Constitution is called a constituting *apud acta*, though it be only done in the absence of the Judge; also the parties and attornies interested when they are in different places, may constitute Proctors before a Notary Publick, and may stipulate as above, in his presence and before witnesses, and may demand of him to draw up a publick declaration and cause it to be recorded. In this last case the Proctors usually say " I exhibit my Proxy for A. B. taken under publick instrument," &c.

[[10] The original is thus:—*et in signum ejusdem accipiet constituentem ac stipulantem per manum dextram, &c.* I at first thought, that this meant simply the signature of the party, but when we reflect upon the ignorance of the early ages, when few could write, we are led to conclude that taking by the hand or other symbols, supplied the place of signatures. As in some of the States, in taking a recognizance, our Prothonotaries and Justices say, *are you content?—Tr.*]

Additions to Title 8.

[The next thing considerable in order, seems to be the Proctor, his office and power, &c.— Seeing no citation though executed, can be brought into Court but by the Proctor, nor any notice taken of it, unless exhibited by him.— Therefore, among the several divisions of Proctors (in respect of their offices) we shall only make use of that definition best fitting our purpose; and in this place it is *Procurator Judicialis*, a Judicial Proctor,[11] which is intended; (that is) he who manages any one's concern in a Court of Judicature, by the special mandate of his client. The division of Judicial Proctors, see in *Myn. Inst. de action.* F. 10.

How and when Proctors may be substituted.

1. What a substitution is and the several kinds of it.
2. When a Proctor may substitute another in his stead in any cause.

1. A substitution is the putting any one in his stead, giving power to act in his absence. There are several sorts of substitutions; some are testamentary[12] (which are likewise general or spe-

[11 Fide Procur. *l.* 1. 1. 71. 1. 72. Cod. Eodem Urum, disput. 3. th. 1. n. 2. Jac. Bouric. de officio Advocati, c. 1, 2. Specul. Noctit. in rub. Eodem n. 1. Wesemb. ff. de Procur. n. 1. 2.—*Tr.*]

[12 A testamentary substitution in the Civil Law, is the limitation of an estate by will, to go from one person to another upon a certain contingency. The *pupil-*

cial) others pupillary : others such as are made by the officers or assistants in Courts of controversy, which agrees properly with the definition here mentioned.

2. And though a Proctor has power given by his proxy to substitute any other in the cause, so often as he shall be absent from the Court; yet he cannot substitute any Proctor before the contesting of suit, called the *litis contestatio*,[13] because he is not, 'till then, lord of the suit, or controversy, nor can it properly be called a suit. But after this *litis contestatio* or contesting of suit, all things whatsoever acted or done by the substituted Proctor, are valid and good in law as if done by the original Proctor. *Wesemb. ubi. s.*

When a Proctor is said to cease to be a Procter in a cause and when not.

The general rule is, *unumquodque dissolvi eodem modo quo colligatum est;* every thing

---

lary substitution is a devise to a minor and in case he dies under age, then to his father, guardian, or other person under whose care or custody he is. These are very little connected with the substitution by a letter or warrant of Attorney; but the Civilians are fond of reducing under one head all matters in which their ingenuity can discover the slightest degree of analogy. *Tr.*]

[13 This is analogous to our Common Law pleadings or joining issue. But no critical nicety is required in these Civil Law pleadings; it is sufficient that they are clear and perspicuous and free from impertinent or irrelevant matter. The parties are at liberty to make as many points or questions of fact or law as may be deemed necessary or proper, so that the cause may be heard and determined upon its real merits.—*Tr.*]

ought to be dissolved after the same manner, as it received its being; so that a Proctor (being constituted by mutual consent) may likewise be released after the same manner. But this general rule admits of several limitations, though before the suit is contested (in which state the Civilians term the business to be *uti res integra*) the Proctor may be revoked or changed: the several causes of revocation are at large enumerated by *Wesemb*.

Likewise the client dying before the suit is contested, though the Proctor has exhibited his proxy, and accepted the libel, &c. yet he needs not further defend the suit, but may let his adversary call the executor or administrators of his deceased client, and begin the suit anew, if any action be against them for that fact; but it is otherwise if the matter ceases to be *integra* or whole, that is, if the suit has been contested. And on the contrary, if the Proctor dies after the suit is contested, the mandate is absolutely revoked,[14] though the substitution made by that Proctor, after the suit so contested, is not absolutely revoked by the death of the party substituting. Also the proxy is said to be revoked when the instance is ended, (viz.) sentence being given in a cause, and a protestation of an appeal being interposed;[15] nor can the Proctors or either party, act or do any thing except they exhibit their proxy for their client anew, after the sentence is laid, which often happens when the

[14 Ranch. ad Guid. papam, p. 119.—*Tr.*]
[15 Wesemb. ubi. *S.* Berlachin. repert. verbo procuror appellans verbis qui eum item verbis. p. 234.—*Tr.*]

Proctor appealing comes before the Judge (from whom he appeals) and alleges, that he has so appealed, and desires dismission, &c. or where the party who got the cause comes and demands sentence to be put in execution. And though the appellate do obtain sentence of remission, and do present this letter of remission to the Judge from whom it was appealed; yet he can do nothing in the presence of his adversary's Proctor, but must call the principal party by new process, in like manner whether it is appealed or not. After sentence is given, the party who got the sentence, must call the adverse party by way of process, to see the sentence put in execution and both of them must constitute their Proctors as at first. But if the principal party die after the suit has been contested by the Proctors, the Proctor of that party so dying (whether plaintiff or defendant) is (by the contestation of suit, *res nimirum desinens esse integra*, as the civil law calls it) made lord of the suit,[16] and may prosecute and defend the suit, and do all things which ought to have been done, if the principal party had been alive; and likewise obtain a definitive sentence. But we must distinguish between real and personal actions, for all actions that are personal[17] do die with the person: such as are actions or causes for defamation or matrimonial, and such like; but in

---

[16 Zouch Elem. Jur. p. 5. Sect. 8. Sect. et procuror. *Tr.*]

[17 Inst. Sect. ovum. de Succes. Myns. Grav. ad vest. *Tr.*]

real actions, which may respect the goods, or the right any one pretends to a personal estate, &c. then what is above said takes place. Likewise, if any appeal from any pretended grievance which they suffer in the proceedings, before the definitive sentence, and the Judge, to whom it was appealed, pronounceth, that it was unjustly appealed, and thereupon remits the cause back to the Judge from whom it was appealed, and the party appellate exhibits the letters remissary before the Judge from whom, &c. and makes request that they may proceed according to the former acts,[18] and in the same state in which the cause was at the time of the appeal; in this case, the Proctor of the party appellate, may, in the presence of the Proctor who appealed, act and do all things as if he had not been appealed at all. For the Proctor of the appealing party does not cease to be Proctor; if the appeal be made from some grievances committed after the contesting of suit, but before the sentence, seeing the procuratory mandate is of force until the definitive sentence. And thence it happens, that the party appellate needs not (in this sort of remission) call the principal party who appealed, to see further proceedings, as above. Cons. Prac. 30.]

[18 Gail l. 1. obs. 109. n. 3, 4, 5. &c.   Grav. ad vest. l. 4. c. 4. n. 39. verbo nisi forte.—*Tr.*]

Tit. 9. *The petition of the Plaintiff's Proctor at the time of the return of the Warrant before the Judge.*

The Proctor for the plaintiff appears before the Judge saying as follows :[19]

" I exhibit my proxy in writing, (or *apud acta*, if he was thus constituted) for N. (*i. e.* for the plaintiff) and make myself party to the same; and I exhibit the original mandate with the certificate indorsed thereon, (or, upon the execution of which the mandatory here present in Court attests by his oath.) And I accuse M. of contumacy because he was bound to make his legal appearance here this day, (as well by the tenour of the mandate, as by the stipulation or undertaking of his bail-bond which was executed in this behalf and remains in the hands of the Registrar, or, which is now ready to be exhibited by me) and is not now forthcoming."

" Wherefore I pray that he be declared in contumacy, and that, in pain of such contu-

---

[[19] By this and other titles in Clerke we learn that in the early stage of jurisprudence, the pleadings were oral in the Civil, as well as in the Common Law Courts. But a different practice has since been introduced, and every thing in the course of a Civil Law suit, except incidental motions, is now exhibited in writing in the various forms of Libels, Petitions, Allegations, Answers, Replications, Duplications, &c. which are not required to be framed in any formal set of words. These formularies, however are curious, as contributing to show the ancient practice of the Courts of Civil Law in England, and through them, as though our ancient Common Law Courts, important principles may still be traced, which will be found useful to the modern practitioner.—*Tr.*]

macy, he be declared to have incurred the forfeit of his bond."

Then the Judge shall order the defendant to be thrice called upon his stipulation by the Marshal of the Court, and in case he does not appear, he shall pronounce the bond to be forfeited, and order him to be taken into custody until the penalty be paid. When the defendant fails to appear, the Judge is accustomed to allow a reasonable proportion of the penalty thus forfeited, to the plaintiff, in consequence of the injury which he may sustain by the delay in his suit. He may dispose of the remainder according to his discretion;* for the aforesaid stipulation for the appearance of the defendant was said to be a prætorian stipulation,[20] and is, therefore, at the disposal of the Judge. But in case the defendant, notwithstanding the stipulation for his appearance, does not appear, but flies the Kingdom or dies, leaving no effects, then the whole amount of the stipulation entered into by the fidejussores for his appearance, is to be delivered to the plaintiff upon his making proof of the debt.

---

* Nam tota Summa foris facta, debetur Domino Admirallo, quia cautio, illi interponitur non parti.

[[20] *Prætorian* stipulation is made to the Court, *conventual* to the party. The bail are not discharged by the surrender or death of the principal, as at Common Law. In proceedings *in personam*, the caution for the appearance of the party is prætorian.—*Tr.*]

Tit. 10. *The petition* of the defendant upon perfecting his legal appearance according to the stipulation, and the plaintiff not appearing or neglecting to prosecute his suit.*

If the defendant appear according to the arrest and the bail which was put in by others for him, he, or his Proctor in exhibiting his proxy, in writing or *apud acta*, shall say:

" I allege that M. here present in Court was and is arrested according to the Warrant or mandate which was issued from this Court, and that he has given bail for his appearance here this day, to answer the complaint of N. in a certain civil and maritime cause. But that the said N. the plaintiff, neither appears in person nor by his Proctor, and neglects to prosecute his cause; and moreover that my client is ready to produce proper and sufficient securities to respond to the plaintiff in the said action by him commenced, according to the provisions of the law and the rules of this Court. Wherefore, I pray that my client may be hence dismissed with costs, and that his bail-bond be decreed to be returned to him or be cancelled."

Then the Judge shall cause the Plaintiff to be publickly called by the Marshal of the Court, and in default of his personal appearance, or by his Proctor, and on account of his utter negligence to prosecute his suit, the Judge in his discretion, may pass such a decree as has been

---

* Vide Gail. lib. 1. obs. 59. per totum. Et vid. Clerke's Prax. in Caus. Eccl. Tit. 53. per Oughtonum.

prayed on the part of the defendant, and condemn the plaintiff in costs, or that he shall not be heard at any future day unless the defendant's costs are discharged : or he may grant a continuance of the cause until some future Court day, and then decree as above : or he may decree that the plaintiff be called at a future day under the penalty of being finally dismissed with costs, which is the more usual course.

But this is to be observed here; if the defendant have his bail in Court, ready to answer to the plaintiff in the particular cause, and believes that the plaintiff will appear before the day which has been granted for his appearance, or on the very day on which he may be cited to appear, and prosecute the suit ; then he, the defendant, may for fear of surprise, enter his security at once, lest he might not have them ready on the day appointed for the plaintiff's appearance, and his bail-bond should be decreed to be forfeited. And then a bill of costs is to be made out and taxed by the Judge, and the party is to swear to the disbursement of the said costs. But of the taxing of costs: the monition for the payment of them and other incidental expenses, is to be proceeded on as in Ecclesiastical Courts; with this difference, that in the Ecclesiastical Courts the party who is condemned in costs is admonished to pay them by a certain day, otherwise to appear on another day and show cause why he should not be excommunicated; whereas, in the Admiralty, in civil and maritime causes, the monition contains an injunction to the party to pay the costs by a certain day mentioned therein, and there is moreover inserted in a *capias* clause, by which, if he does not pay them on or before that day, the officer is ordered to take his body and commit him to prison until he shall pay.*

Tit. 11. *The Petition of the Proctors* hinc indè, *if both parties appear.*

If the plaintiff appear at the day appointed either in person or by his Proctor, he shall say, " I accuse the defendant of contumacy, &c." (as in Tit. 9.) Then the defendant, if he appear in person or by his Proctor, shall pray that a libel and fidejussory security† be given by the opposite party, or that he be dismissed with costs.

‡The Proctor for the plaintiff shall reply, that, first he prays that proper fidejussory security be put in by the defendant according to the provisions of law and the forms of the Court, to the effect specified in Tit. 12.

Then the Judge shall say " We direct that both parties shall file their fidejussory security by to-morrow, and that the plaintiff file his libel on the same day.

---

* Vid. Cler. Prax. in Curiis Eccles. Tit. 27. 28. 29. per Oughtonum.

† Although the Laws require that the plaintiff shall put in security by proper fidejussores before he corrects his libel, yet it is little attended to in Courts. addit. ad Capel. Tholos. quæs. 138.

‡ For the plaintiff is not bound to libel, unless fidejussory security has been first put in by the defendant.

Tit. 12. *Of the fidejussory security given by the defendant, and the stipulation which is entered into by him.*

*The defendant ought to find at least two fidejussores, who should be bound respectively to the plaintiff, in the sum for which the action was instituted, to these effects,† viz : to abide the sentence, *(judicio sisti)* to pay costs, and to ratify the acts of the Proctor by him constituted, or to be constituted. But if it be objected, on the part of the defendant, that the plaintiff has maliciously commenced his action for a greater sum than is really due to him, in order that the defendant might be cast into prison for want of fidejussores; the Judge, for the prevention of such fraud or rather malice, may compel the plaintiff to swear to the sum which he expects to prove is due to him, and the fidejussory caution shall be taken to that amount :[21] the other disbursements incurred by praying the decision of the Judge, and for expenses in supporting the cause, if the plaintiff succeeds, are to be added.

---

* Vid Digest. Lib. 46. Tit. 7. l. 9. But after decree pronounced, are the fidejussores held to that which may be pronounced in the Appeal cause ? Vid. l. 20. *cum apud ;* where it is said they are not unless there be another action. Vid. Bart. add. l. et etiam Castrens. ib.

† Ridley's View, pars 2. c. 1. §. 5. in fine.

[21 This seems now to be made unnecessary by the rule, 28th Jan. 1801, requiring an affidavit of the debt before the Warrant issues. 2 Bro. Civ. & Adm. 410. *Tr.*]

Tit. 13. *The Petition and Protest of the Proctor for the Plaintiff at the introduction of fidejussores of this kind.*

As it sometimes happens that the defendant introduces fidejussores who are unknown, or who are not able to pay the amount sued for, the Proctor for the plaintiff, at the production of them, may protest against the admission or reception of them and their insufficiency, and he may pray for more ample security. This protestation is particularly necessary, because, if it be neglected, the party is excluded from demanding more substantial security at any future period of the cause.

Tit. 14. *The production of fidejussores on the part of the plaintiff.*

* The plaintiff is also obliged to find fidejussores to these effects, viz. for the prosecution of the suit; for the payment of the defendant's costs if the plaintiff fail in his cause,† and for the production of the plaintiff personally as often as he may be called. For take notice, that the plaintiff can use the personal answers of the

---

* Vid. Capell. Tholos. decis. 138. nu. 3. vid. auth. generaliter Cod. de Episc. et Cleric. vid. Fachsii differentias Juris Civilis et Saxonici, Lib. 1. Tit. 40. p. 154. Novell. 111. 2. Oldendorp. Class. 1. Act. 7. in fine.

† Cave. For unless you add, *in which the plaintiff shall be condemned,* the fidejussores will be bound to pay costs though the plaintiff may not be condemned in costs. Thus Salicet. l. in the conclusion of Cod. de fruct. et lit. Expens. nu. 2. versic; and therefore be careful.

defendant, to the allegations contained in the libel, or any other matter by him suggested and filed. So it is lawful for the defendant to make use of the personal answers of the plaintiff, to any matter of defence, whether by exceptions or by any other kind of allegations whatsoever, which are by him put in. And it is proper that the Proctor for the defendant should dissent and protest at the time of taking the fidejussores for the plaintiff, in the same manner as was done by the plaintiff in the preceding title.

TIT. 15. *The Petition of the Proctor for better or more substantial security.*

* ALTHOUGH fidejussory caution has been put in on both sides, yet if any of the fidejussores are not sufficient, the Proctor for the adverse party may object to them, either at the contestation of the claim or after the conclusion of the cause, in these words:

---

* When the security is prætorian or judicial, upon the death of one of the fidejussores, or upon the event of his becoming insolvent, the party may demand additional security—secus, when the security is conventional, vid. l. si ab arbitro. 10. §. ult. Dig. qui satisdare tenent. et Alber. et Angel. et Jas. ibidem in 8 Not. Vincent. de Franchis. decis. 480.

[In the Admiralty they do not take recognizances, because not being a court of record, a prohibition would lie. This seems to be the law at present, though there has been much dispute upon the subject. See Zouch, Godolphin, and Lord Rayne, 1285, 1. Bro. Civ. & Adm. 361, says that the securities or stipulations taken in the Court of Admiralty, in the nature of bail have no priority over specialty debts, nor do they affect laws. Nor is the heir bound by them unless expressly mentioned, but the executor is.—*Tr.*]

"I allege that N. and M. fidejussores produced on the part of R. in this cause, were not nor are sufficient, according to the matter in dispute; and that the said fidejussores, or such a particular one, is commonly held and reputed among his neighbours and acquaintance to be a poor man, especially as not worth such a sum, or even a much less sum than that for which he is bound. Therefore I pray that better and more substantial security be given by the adverse party, or that he be taken into custody until such security be given by him."

Then the Proctor for the opposite side shall say:

" I dissent and protest the nullity of this petition, and I deny the truth of the allegations contained in it: and I allege that the fidejussores in behalf of my client in this cause, are good and sufficient, and that they are able to pay the amount of the sum for which this cause has been instituted, and as such they are commonly accounted and esteemed. Therefore I pray that may client be not required to put in additional security in this cause."*

---

* And note, that although the fidejussores put in by the defendant were sufficient at the time when they were received as such, yet, if they afterwards become *lapsi facultatibus*, as it is said above, the defendant is bound to give other and better security. Likewise if the fidejussores who were introduced at the commencement of the cause, cease, during its pendency, to be sufficient, the party, in whose behalf they were introduced, ought to give others.

Tit. 16. *The decree of the Judge on the petition for further security.*

This matter or question, viz. whether the fidejussores are proper and sufficient or not, the Judge ought and he usually does decide upon summary proof, in order to prevent any delay of the principal cause and further expense to the parties, and if he be able to ascertain immediately by any persons present in Court, (for on Court days merchants are usually there, who are generally acquainted with the circumstances of the citizens, and often they are known to the Judge himself) he shall order the party to produce further and more sufficient security by some future day. But if the premises be not proved, the Judge shall assign a time for hearing his determination.

Tit. 17. *The form of proving the sufficiency or insufficiency of the fidejussores.*

Summary and not full or exact proof is required in such a case: Thus, if the party alleging the insufficiency of the fidejussores, produce to the Judge, a certificate under the hand of the King's Collector of the Revenue in those parts in which the fidejussores dwell, that they do not pay their taxes, or, at least, not as much as they are rated at, or if from the certificate of honest men of the neighbourhood who are known to the Judge, it appear that these men are publickly held and reputed to be poor, or, at least, not worth as much as the amount for which they are security, or a sum much less than that for which the action was instituted, the Judge should decree as above in Title 16. But, on the contrary, if the party which produced the fidejussores, shall prove in the manner abovementioned, or by any other kind of proof, that his fidejussory caution is good and sufficient, then the aforesaid petition for the introduction of new security is to be refused, either in express terms, or tacitly by proceeding in a manner contrary to it.

TIT. 18. *The security to be interposed by the principal party to indemnify his fidejussores.*

AT the same time and in the same record in which the stipulation or recognizance of the fidejussores was taken, as in Title 12. the principal party enters into an obligation to a similar effect with that for which the fidejussores are bound, and also to indemnify them against the consequence of their security. And this caution of the principal party ought to be taken in double the amount of the fidejussory caution, or, at least, in a greater sum than that in which they are bound, at the discretion of the Judge.

TIT. 19. *The giving or tendering a libel.*

AFTER the exhibiting and introduction of the fidejussory caution, *hinc inde*, to the effect specified in Title 12. the Proctor for the plaintiff shall say:

" I give you a libel and pray decree for proceeding in a plain and summary manner."

As all civil and maritime causes are summary,* the mode of proceeding is the same as in Ecclesiastical cases,† viz. there is to be a decree for the appearance of the principal party; a probatory term is to be limited or assigned: the principal is to be produced: the witnesses are to be brought into Court: a commission for the examination of witnesses is to be issued, if they are within the Kingdom, or, if they are not, a commission *sub mutuæ vicissitudinis*, from the mutual aid granted by different jurisdictions for the furtherance of justice: that commission is to be proceeded in and duly certified: the publication of the testimony is to be prayed and decreed: and finally, the course of proceedings until pronouncing the final sentence is to be the same as in the Ecclesiastical Courts with the exceptions which shall hereafter be shown.

---

* Summatìm, brevitèr ac de plane citrà strepitum forensem, levato velo, *i. e.* aperto ostio, cui velum solebat prætendi Locc. Lib. 3. c. 11. §. 2. Welwood Tit. 5. f. 53.

Causa maturanda ob navigandi necessitatem, cujus periculum est in morâ. Locc. Lib. 3. c. 11. §. 2.

Maximè in causis de submersis navibus aut naufragiis. Cod. 11. 55. Locc. Lib. 3. c. 11. 2. Of wreck or Spoil. Welw. Tit. 5. f. 53.

Insomuch that they need not put up their petitions in writing. Welm. Tit. 5. f. 54.

In Admiralitats Hollandiæ duplica non est litigautibus permissa. Locc. Lib. 3. c. 11. §. 2.

In liquidis delictis Nauticis summariè et executivè procedendum per jura Sueciæ Locc. Lib. 3. c. 11. §. 2.

† Vid. Clerk. Prac. in causis Ecc. Tit. 61. 58. 80. 76. 86. 65. 62. 97. 95. 96. 71. &c. 221. per Oughtonum.

Additions to Title 19.

[A TERM PROBATORY, is said to be that time, or delay which was given to the plaintiff wherein he might prove what he pleads or sueth for; nor has the plaintiff the sole or absolute benefit of it: for the defendant may likewise make use of this term, if the plaintiff renounce it.

Now proofs are said to be twofold, in respect of the matter in controversy. One sort of proof has relation to the matters of fact, the other has relation to the matters of law which occur therein; and this latter sort ought to be made by the laws, customs, canons, &c. Sometimes directly, sometimes by argument. *Mascardus* de proba. vol. 1. 94. 3. Wesemb. in paratit. ff. de proba et pres..n. 2.

PROOFS[*] which have relation to the fact are said to be either

- *Most evident*, which are such as are made by instruments of undoubted credit, &c.
- *Evident and clear*, or full proof which makes so much as serves to determine the suit; and this is done either by

  witnesses, i. e. writings, confession, evidence of the fact, an oath, a just presumption, fame, or undoubted circumstances.

or

- *Less evident*,[†] which make some proof of the matter, but not so much as will ground a sentence upon; this is made by

  one witness, a private book, or writing, a mean, reasonable, or indifferent presumption.

---

[*] De hisce prob. apud Liud. videas t. dejure jur. c. Presbyteri. Sect. quod Si verb. probationes.

[†] Mascard. de prob. vol 1. quest. 4. n. 16 Ummius disp 15 th. 1 alc. ubi. s. et in tract. presumption. in prin. par. 3. n. 2. Wesemb. in f. f. de prob. & pres. n. 4 ubi plene de his probation. divisionibus reperias. Speculator tit. de prob. sect. videndum.

Commissions Submutuæ Vicissitudinis, or Letters Rogatory.

By the Law of Nations, the Courts of Justice of different countries are bound to be mutually aiding and assisting to each other for the furtherance of justice. Hence, when the testimony of witnesses who reside abroad is necessary in a cause, the Court or Tribunal where the action is pending, may send to the Court or Tribunal within whose jurisdiction the witnesses reside, a writ patent or close, as they may think proper. They are usually called *letters rogatory*, but our author here denominates them *sub mutuæ vicissitudinis*,* from a clause which they generally contain. By that instrument the Court abroad is informed that a certain claim is pending in which the testimony of certain witnesses who reside within its jurisdiction is required, and it is requested to take their depositions or cause them to be taken, in due course and form of law for the furtherance of justice and *sub mutuæ vicissitudinis obtentu*: that is with an offer on the part of the Court making the request to do the like for the other in a similar case. If these Letters Rogatory are received by an inferior Judge, he proceeds to call the witnesses before him, by the process commonly employed within his jurisdiction, examines them on interrogatories or takes their depositions, as the case may be,

---

* Vid. the form of Letters Rogatory in Clerke's Ecc. Prac. Tit. 167. p. 236.

and the proceedings being filed in the Registry of his Court, authentick copies thereof, duly certified, are transmitted to the Court *à quo*, and are legal evidence in the cause. If the letters are directed to a Court of superior jurisdiction, they appoint an examiner or commissioners for the purpose of executing them and the proceedings are filed and returned in the same manner.

Such is the manner in which the Courts of those countries of Europe which are governed by the Civil Law, proceed with regard to each other. In former times, even the Courts of Common Law in England availed themselves of this privilege of calling upon the Courts of other countries for their assistance. Thus, in the reign of Edward I. in an action of trespass for a ship and cargo, *Letters Rogatory* issued from the Court where the action was pending directed to the Count of Holland, requesting him to cause an inquest to be taken by good and lawful men of his own country, to ascertain what goods, wares, and merchandizes had been shipped on board the vessel in question. 1. Ro. Ab. 530. pl. 13.

By the Judiciary Act, (Laws U. S. vol. 1. p. 47) the mode of proof by oral testimony and examination of witnesses in open Court, is the same in all the Courts of the United States, as well in the trial of causes in equity and of admiralty and maritime jurisdiction, as of actions at Common Law. When the testimony of any person is necessary in a civil cause depending in one of these Courts, who lives at a greater distance from the place of trial than one hundred miles, or is bound on a voyage to sea, or is about to go out of the United States, or out of the District in which the Court is held, and to a greater distance than one hundred miles, before the time of trial, or if he be ancient and infirm, his deposition may be taken *de bene esse* before any Judge or Justice of the United States, or before any Chancellor, Justice, or Judge of a Supreme or Superior Court, Mayor, or Chief Magistrate of a City, or Judge of a County Court or Court of Common Pleas of any of the United States. But the person before whom the deposition is taken, must not be of counsel or attorney to either of the parties, nor interested in the event of the cause. In such cases it is necessary that there be a notification from the Magistrate before whom the deposition is to be taken to the adverse party to attend and put interrogatories if he think fit. This must be served on the party or his attorney, as either may be nearer, if either be within one hundred miles of the place of such caption, allowing time for their attendance after being notified, not less than at the rate of one day, Sundays exclusive, for every twenty miles travel.

In causes of Admiralty and maritime jurisdistion, or other cases of seizure, when a libel is filed, in which an adverse party is not named, and the depositions of persons in the circumstances above described, are taken before a claim has been put in, this notification is to be given to the person who has the agency or possession of the property libelled at the time of the capture or seizure, if known to the libellant.

Every person thus deposing must be carefully examined and cautioned, and sworn or affirmed to testify the whole truth. The testimony must be reduced to writing only by the Magistrate, or the deponent in his presence, and must be subscribed by the latter. The depositions are to be retained by the Magistrate until he shall deliver it with his own hand into the Court for which they were taken, or they must be sealed up together by the Magistrate, with the reasons of their being taken, and of the notice, if any, which has been given, and remain under his seal until opened in Court. Any person may be compelled to appear and testify before a Magistrate in the same manner as he might be compelled to appear in Court for the same purpose.

In the trial of any cause of Admiralty and maritime jurisdiction, from the decision of which it is lawful to appeal, if either party satisfy the Court, that probably it will not be in his power to produce the witnesses who are there testifying, before the Circuit Court should an appeal be had, and move that their testimony be taken down in writing, it is done by the Clerk of the Court. This testimony may be used on the trial of the appeal, if it appear to the satisfaction of the Court, that the witnesses are then dead or gone out of the United States, or to a greater distance than one hundred miles from the place where the Court is sitting, or that by reason of age, sickness, bodily infirmity or imprisonment, they are unable to travel and appear at Court, and not otherwise. The Courts of the United States have full power to grant a *dedimus potes-*

tatem to take depositions according to common usage, when it may be necessary to prevent a failure or delay of justice. The Circuit Court, in the same manner as a Court of equity, according to the usages in chancery may direct depositions *in perpetuam rei memoriam* to be taken as to matters which are cognizable in any Courts of the United States.

It is to be regretted that the principle of the Civil Law with respect to Letters Rogatory, has not been introduced into our practice. Commissions of *dedimus potestatem* are liable to great objections. It is sometimes difficult to procure the names of commissioners and when they are obtained, it is often impossible to prevail upon them to act. They have no power to compel the attendance of witnesses, and as they rarely receive a compensation for their services, they do not care much about attending themselves. Thus the return of the commission is protracted, the Attorney is unable to account for the delay, his opponent is ordered to press for a trial, and an honest creditor is frequently deprived of a just claim. This is far from being an exaggerated picture. We may add that the witnesses cannot be prosecuted for perjury before the tribunals of their own country, nor, while they remain there, can they be prosecuted in that in which the cause was tried. It often happens, too, that the constituted authorities of the place, consider these commissions as an encroachment upon their jurisdiction, and refuse to permit them to be executed. Instances of this kind have sometimes happened in cases of commissions which have been issued by the Courts of the United States, the commissioners having been threatened with punishment if they proceeded to act under them.

These and other inconveniences have been sensibly felt by practitioners, who have long wished that something more effectual for the advancement of justice were introduced into our practice. In more modern times the practice of issuing Letters Rogatory has fallen into disuse in the English Courts of Common Law and commissions of *Dedimus potestatum* have offered a feeble substitute. But, however, it may be with respect to the Courts of Common Law, whose practice does not properly fall within the scope of our present inquiry, the principle is fully established in England, that Courts of Admiralty in different countries are to be mutually aiding and assisting to each other, and are ever bound to execute the judgments of each other. The reason which is given, is that they all proceed by the same system of jurisprudence, the Civil Law. 1 Vent. 32. 1 Ro. Abr. 530. 1 Lev. 267. 1 Sid. 418. 2 Keb. 511. 610. 1 Show. 143. 2 Show. 232. Skin. 59. Raym. 473. 2 Ld. Raym. Danv. abr. 265.

Hence it follows, that Letters Rogatory, or a Commission *sub mutuæ vicissitudinis*, may issue from an Admiralty Court in the United States, to a Court of the same nature abroad, for the purpose of taking the depositions of witnesses, or even of executing their own judgments; and it appears also to follow, that if Letters Rogatory come from a Court or Tribunal of a foreign country, directed as they usually are, to the Judge of a particular place, without any designation, the District Judge, having Admiralty jurisdiction is the proper person to cause them to be complied with.—*Tr.*]

TIT. 20. *The manner of certifying the decree to answer the allegations of the Libel, if the defendant cannot be cited.*

ALTHOUGH every original warrant or mandate contains an arrest of the person of the defendant, yet the decree, or as it is called, the personal warrant to the principal party, to answer the charges comprized in the libel, ought to contain only a citation, like the decree to the principal party in Ecclesiastical causes. But if the defendant abscond, so that a citation cannot be served upon him personally, it is to be certified by the mandatory himself in person upon oath, or by an authentick certificate as in Ecclesiastical causes. And a decree is to be prayed and passed in manner and form against the principal party to the effect above mentioned, viz. to appear on a certain competent day at the pleasure of the Judge. Upon the return of this citatory mandate,[22] if the defendant do not appear, a decree against the fidejussores is to be prayed, directing them to produce the body of the prin-

---

[22 This practice seems to be contrary to the Civil Law, which requires that the goods of the absconding person should be seized before a decree can be passed against the fidejussores. Did. Lib. 42. Tit. 4. l. 2. *Quibus ex causis in possessionem eatur.*—*Tr.*]

cipal under pain of the penalty into which they have entered.

Yet it is usual for the Judge, at least in the causes of poor people, if the defendant cannot be cited against the day mentioned in the citatory mandate, because he is concealed, to decree that the fidejussores be called by a certain competent day, to produce the body of the principal party for the aforesaid purposes under pain of their stipulation by a certain day, which is to be assigned at the pleasure of the Judge.

TIT. 21. *The manner of executing the aforesaid Warrant* viis et modis.

THE mandatory shall go to the accustomed place of residence of the party who is sued, and shall cite him personally, if possible. But if he cannot apprehend him, he may serve the citation in this manner: he shall affix it upon the door of his house, or upon the gates of the Parish church on a dominical day, or during the unemployed time of divine service; or if the defendant be a merchant of London, or have no certain domicil, he may affix it upon the publick Royal Exchange, where a great crowd of merchants is accustomed to resort. And the officer is bound to affix a true copy of this kind of citatory mandate at the door, gate, or Exchange, as we have said. Likewise, if the fidejussores be concealed, so that they cannot be cited to the foregoing effects, a decree *viis et modis* is to be passed against them, following the manner and form as has been before directed, against the principal when he absconds.

ADDITIONS TO TITLE 21.

[And this it is which is called *citatio viis et modis*, or *citatio publica*, a public citation, being executed either by publick edict (a copy thereof being affixed to the doors of the house where the defendant dwells, or the doors of the church within whose Parish he inhabits) or (as my author tells me) by publication in the church in time of divine service; or *per campanam*, the tolling of a bell ; or *per tubam*, the sounding of a trumpet; *et vexilli erectionem*. This being done, a certificate must be made of the premises, and the citation brought into Court (as is even now mentioned) and if the party cited appear not, the plaintiff's Proctor must accuse his contumacy, (he being first three times called by the crier of the Court) and in penalty of such his contumacy, he must request that he may be excommunicated. Cons. Prac. p. 35.]

TIT. 22. *The Petition of the Proctor for the Plaintiff, when the fidejussores on the part of the defendant being monished to bring in the principal, neither appear themselves, nor have him forthcoming.*

THE Proctor for the plaintiff shall say :
" I exhibit your original mandate, together with a certificate indorsed, (or, to the execution

of which the mandatory here present in Court maketh oath) and I accuse of contumacy X and Y, the fidejussores on the part of the defendant who were ordered to produce him in Court this day, to answer, in person, the positions which are contained in the libel: otherwise to appear personally here this day, by producing the principal party to abide the aforesaid effects, according to the stipulation by them interposed; or to show cause why they should not be declared to have incurred this forfeiture or penal stipulation.* Wherefore I pray that they may be decreed contumacious, and in pain of their contumacy that they be declared to have incurred this forfeiture; and I pray that they be ordered to stand committed until the said forfeiture shall be paid."

Then the Marshal is to make publick proclamation for the aforesaid fidejussores, and upon their failure to appear, they are to be pronounced contumacious, in pain whereof they have incurred the forfeiture and are to be committed until it is paid. Yet this is to be noted, that it is not usual for the Judge, although he does possess the power, to pass this decree on the first day appointed for the appearance of the fidejussores; but to wait one or two Court days and to continue their appearance. If this be done, the Proctor for the plaintiff should take care, that the certificate of the warrant introduced by the fidejussores be also continued, in order that,

---

* Dig. Lib. 2. Tit. 8. c. 2. §. ult. Qui satisdare cogantur, &c.

if on the same day the fidejussores do not obey the mandate, (that is, if they fail to have the principal party forthcoming) he may immediately charge them with contumacy and pray as before.* And note,† that if the principal party should appear within one or another day (intrà unum aut *alterum* diem) after the interposition of the decree against the fidejussores that they have incurred the penalty of their stipulation, and are about to be committed, and before that decree has been executed upon them, the Judge may moderate the penalty or forfeiture, notwithstanding his decree.‡ But it must be done in such a manner that a part of the sum thus mo-

---

* Vid Clerke's Prax. in Caus. Ecc. Title 70. per Oughtonum.

† When a person has stipulated any thing under any certain penalty, as, if within a certain time he shall not produce a defendant, or if that time being elapsed the penalty shall be forfeited, Justinian still relieves the fidejussor so far as not to exact the penalty immediately, but after a certain time, within which he may purge the delay, by producing the defendant, or by making defence for him. *Farinac. pars* 1. *a prax. crimin. quæs.* 34. *n.* 135. *Gœddæus in l.* 12. *Digest. de Verb. Signif. V.* 1. *nu.* 12. *Perez. prœlect. in Cod. de fidejuss. n.* 18. Which he could not otherwise obtain, because, regularly, no excuse nor subterfuge will avail to prevent the forfeiture of the penalty on the day prescribed by the obligation; nor is there any necessity for further interposing or monition, when, that day being added, the party is sufficiently justified in requiring the fulfilment of the engagement. *Zas. ad l. si insulam Dig. de Verb. Oblig.*

‡ Because the security is Prætorian. Prætorian Stipulations are favourably received *gl. in l. sancimus Cod. de fidejuss. in verb. pecunias. Vid. Card. Mant. lib.* 16. *Tit.* 20. *n.* 17. *Zas. in l. insulam Dig. de Verb. nu.* 21. *et* 24.

derated shall be given to the plaintiff, on account of the delay and the expenses of his cause.

Tit. 23. *The petition of the fidejussores if they appear on the day appointed for them, to bring in the principal party.*

Actions which are instituted in the Court of Admiralty, are generally between merchants, as well foreign as domestick, and masters and mariners. Therefore if the principal party, for the appearance of whom the fidejussores are summoned, be absent from the kingdom at the time when he should be produced, the fidejussores are bound to appear in order to purge themselves of contumacy, by stating the cause of the impediment, as the absence or illness of the principal, and holding themselves ready and willing to bring him in, on some future competent day to be assigned by the Judge. And if they make oath of the truth of this allegation,[*] the Judge ought, and he usually does, appoint some future day for the fidejussores to bring in the principal for the aforesaid effect, according to the distance of the residence of the principal.

At this day the Proctor for the plaintiff ought to pray, as above, a continuation of the certificate by him already filed against the aforesaid fidejussores, that if they do not surrender the principal on that day, he may, in pain of their contumacy, demand that they be pronounced

---

[*] Vid. Farinac. Prax. Crimin. par. 1. qu. 34. nu. 147.

to have incurred the penalty of their stipulation, as above, Tit. 22. Also the Proctor for the plaintiff may, *ex abundanti* and for greater caution, pray the Judge that he admonish the *fidejussores*, when they have petitioned and alleged as before mentioned, to appear on the aforesaid day, which was assigned to bring in the principal, that they may hear themselves declared to have incurred the forfeiture, provided they do not produce the principal, in which case the sum of forfeiture may be passed, in pain of their contumacy, even though the aforesaid certificate should not have been continued.

And here two things are to be noted; first, that if the plaintiff or his proctor should suspect that the *fidejussores* demand a deliberatory time to produce the principal, for the purpose of delaying the cause, and that on the day assigned for bringing him in, they intend to allege other frivolous reasons to obtain a second delay or respite for bringing him in, or even then to pray a commission to foreign or distant parts for his examination; he may, on the first day of the appearance of the *fidejussores*, when they pray a deliberatory time to produce the principal, call upon the Judge to compel them, at that time, to have the benefit of a commission to foreign parts or places at a distance from the Court, for the examination of the said defendant, under pain of being deprived of that privilege at a future time. And the Judge, for the prevention of delay, has the power and is accustomed thus to decree.

Secondly, the Judge, for cause or for favour, may admit a Proctor to appear for the *fidejussores*, who may state the reasons which have prevented the appearance of the principal, and pray a time to be assigned for producing him. But in that case, from necessity, the certificate is to be continued to the day appointed for the appearance of the principal, in order that if he do not appear, the Judge may pronounce his decree as above, which could not be done if the certificate had been discontinued.

TIT. 24. *The production of the principal and the punishment to be inflicted upon him if he refuse to submit to an examination under oath.*[25]

IF the principal being cited, should appear to answer the charges contained in the libel, it is to

---

[25 It appears from the whole tenour of this work, that, at the time when it was written, the English Court of Admiralty exercised a much more extensive jurisdiction than it does at present. During the long reign of Elizabeth, in which our authour flourished, we meet with but a single case of a prohibition to the Court of Admiralty and in that their jurisdiction was sustained. Cro. Eliz. 685. It was not until the subsequent reigns of James and Charles I. that a flood of prohibitions, flowing from the enmity which Lord Coke bore towards its jurisdiction, was poured upon that Court. Before that time, it is probable that they took cognizance of every kind of contracts made abroad between or with foreigners. This extent of jurisdiction we find them constantly and strenuously claiming until some time after the Restoration, about which period they appear to have relinquished the unequal contest. *The Aurora*, 3 Rob. 114. *Am. Ed.* This accounts for the circumstance be produced and an oath administered to him, in the same manner and form as in Ecclesiastical causes;* and he is to be admonished to undergo an examination by a day assigned by the Judge, under a certain penalty, sometimes of forty shillings or five pounds, at the will of the Judge and according to the importance of the cause. And if the party does not submit to the examination before the day appointed he is to be charged with contumacy, and to be pronounced to have incurred the aforesaid penalty or mulct; and he is to be committed until he has paid it and submitted to the examination. The money is to be appropriated, at the discretion of the Judge, to pious uses, especially to the relief of poor prisoners, or sometimes to the plaintiff if he be poor, because the process is impeded by the delay of the defendant, to submit to the examination. Yet the Judge is accustomed, *ex gratiâ* to reserve the forfeiture of the party until some future Court-day, before he decrees him to have incurred the penalty and orders him to be arrested.

---

of their principal mode of proceeding, anciently being by capias or warrant against the person, and their ordinary stipulation being *de in judicio sisti*, which is in the nature of our special bail. At present their jurisdiction is almost entirely confined to proceedings *in rem*. The stipulations which are now usually given in the English and American Courts of Admiralty, are *de judicatum solvi*, to abide by the judgment of the Court, and pay the sum which shall be awarded. Hence, the learning of our authour concerning the proceedings which are necessary to fix the bail, when the principal party does not appear, is become almost obsolete.—*Tr.*]

* Clerke's Prax. in Caus. Ecc. Tit. 70. per Oughtonum.

Additions to Title 24.

[If the defendant refuse to take the oath to answer to the positions of the libel, or to any other matter, to which he ought, by law, to answer; or doth pretend any frivolous causes why he ought not to take it, he is not to be pronounced *pro confesso*, as confessing the matter, though he have been after admonished and commanded to take the oath; but he is to be denounced as excommunicated, and is thereupon to be signified to the King's Majesty, and to be imprisoned and there detained, until he take the oath. *Ecc. Pract. P. 3. cap. 3. §. 4. n. 1.*

If the defendant is sworn and do not give a true answer, he may be called again under pain of being pronounced contumacious and declared *pro confesso* " or as one confessing or granting those things, which he refuseth to answer fully to." *ib.* This is called a presumptive confession. *Manual Jur. de verb. signiff. verb. confessio.*

An erroneous confession may be revoked at any time before sentence, provided the errour be made evident. The revocation must be made by the principal party, or by a proctor especially constituted. *Alciat. de confessio.*]

Tit. 25. *The requisition and production of witnesses, and the manner of proceeding if they refuse to be examined.*

WITHIN the probatory term the witnesses are to be required to appear, and their travelling expenses are to be tendered to them. Upon their appearance an oath is to be administered in the form of oaths to witnesses; and they are to be cautioned to submit to an examination under penalty. If they refuse to be examined the same process is to go against them as was before directed against the principal party, in the preceding title.

Addition to Title 25.

[THE witnesses may be required to appear before the Judge or commissioners. *Wesemb.* in *Paratit. Cod. numb.* 5. *lit. D. Scurf. cons.* 9. *num.* 3. *cent.* 1. *Alciat. test. fol.* 148. *Sect. qualiter sint testes producendi.*]

TIT. 26. *Compulsory process against witnesses who are summoned and do not appear.*

UPON the witnesses being summoned and failing to appear, an oath being made of the service of the summons and the tender of travelling expenses, a compulsory process is to be decreed against them to appear by a certain day and take the oath usually sworn by witnesses, and to give testimony in the cause. If they cannot be personally cited, a decree *viis et modis* is to be impetrated: and that is to be executed and certified in the manner and form which is prescribed in Tit. 20, 21. If they do not then appear, a decree or warrant is to be granted for their imprisonment until they submit to be examined.

Tit. 27. *The petition for and issuing of a commission, for the examination of witnesses residing at a distance from the place where the Court sits.*[24]

Before the expiration of the probatory term, if the witnesses dwell at a distance from the seat of judgment, so that they cannot be produced in Court without great expense, and there is danger of a loss of testimony to the litigant parties, a commission is to be prayed and decreed. In the execution of it, the proceedings must be had in the presence of the adverse party or his Attorney, under pain of being declared in contumacy, *in omnibus et per omnia*, as in the Titles which specially treat of these things in *Clerke* Prax. 80. 88. 89. 90. 91. 87. 86. 95. 96. *by Oughton.*

But if the witnesses dwell without the kingdom, which is generally the case in these maritime causes, a commission* *sub mutuæ vicissitudinis obtentu et in juris subsidium*, from the mutual aid granted by different jurisdictions and in support of justice, is to be prayed and granted:

[24 A commission *ad partes*, is a commission to examine witnesses whose places of residence are so distant from that where the Court sits, as to render it inconvenient to have them produced in person. Their depositions are taken by the Registrar or Examiner of the Court, as is usual when they are nigh to the Court.—*Tr.*]

* Vid. Francisci Aretin. consil. 82. quæsito 4º.

Also of the manner and form of praying for this commission and for instructions how to proceed under it agreeably to law, read in the same book, *Tit.* 95. 96. But this is to be noted, that in all commissions of this nature, secular, and not ecclesiastical persons are to be named as commissioners. And they are usually directed when sent beyond sea, to the Judges and Consuls administering Law in the town of N——— Secus, in Ecclesiastical causes, because commissions there must be issued to persons of Ecclesiastical dignity.

ADDITIONS TO TITLE 27.

[The commercial Courts or Tribunals on the continent of Europe were formerly called Consuls. In France, *Judges and Consuls;* in Spain *Priors and Consuls;* in Italy, *Maritime Consuls.* Hence the most ancient work, which is extant, on maritime and commercial law is called, the Consulate of the sea. *Il consolato del mare:* that is, the law or jurisprudence received and admitted in the consular or commercial Courts.— Hence also, commercial agents who are sent from one country to another are called *Consuls,* because they formerly had a consular jurisdiction, or cognizance of all commercial and maritime causes between subjects of their own nation; a power which is still exercised in some countries, by virtue of particular treaties. The Consuls of the United States and France were possessed of this jurisdiction, within the territories of each other, in consequence of provisions to that effect in the consular convention of the 14th Nov. 1788; which became annulled by virtue of the Act of Congress of 7th July, 1798, and has never been since, nor probably ever will be revived.

To these commercial and maritime Courts, therefore, commissions *sub mutuæ* or *letters rogatory* were, in our authour's time, usually directed; and at this day it seems that they might with propriety be directed to the Court, or Judge, of the place to which they are sent, exercising admiralty and maritime jurisdiction.

On the subject of commissions vid. Wesemb. paratit. Cod. num. 5. lit. B. Ruland. de commiss. lib. 1. c. 2. n. 7. Gail 1. obs. 89. n. 3. 96. n. 2. Jacob Blum. proc. Camer. tit. 73. p. 39. Alciatus de position. Sect. quid sit. Fol. 131.

Commissions for the examination of witnesses, in England, run *jointly* and *severally*. Notice is given to both commissioners, and if one absents himself after that notice, the other is at liberty to proceed alone. In the case of the *Ceres*, where one commissioner declined acting in the absence of the other, because he thought he had not power to do so, the Court granted a new commission, but said it was solely on the ground of the refusal to proceed. 3. Rob. Adm. Rep. 107. But in the case of *Guppy* v. *Brown* in Pennsylvania, where a commission had been issued to four, jointly, and was executed and returned by three of them, the defendant's counsel objected to the reading of the depositions and cited 1.

Bac. Abr. 202. 2. Inst. The Court thought the objection fatal, although two of the three who returned the commission were of the defendant's own nomination. 4. Dall. 410.

As far as my experience extends, commissions usually go to three persons with power to any two to act. Many commissions are excluded from being read on account of their not being executed regularly. No precise directions can be given as to the proper manner of executing them, because each State has its peculiar form; but the commissioner can seldom commit an error if he read his authority with care. Each examination should be signed by the deponent and his signature attested by such a number of the commissioners as are rendered necessary to be present at the examination. The expenses of commissions are usually paid by the party at whose instance the commission issued, or in such other manner as has been agreed upon previous to the issuing of them. In the case of *Lynch v. Wood* in Pennsylvania, the plaintiff claimed a variety of expenses which had been incurred in the execution of a commission that had been issued for him *ex-parte*. The Court allowed the charges for swearing the witnesses and for their attendance; but rejected those for agency and for travelling to collect the testimony. 1. Dall. 310.

Under a commission, if a witness disclose a collateral fact to which the inquiry was not directed, the Court will allow a second commission to be issued for the purpose of an examination of that fact 1 New York T. R. 345.

If the notice of an application for a commission contain the names of commissioners, and the party served do not then object he is precluded. *ib.* 5.

A commission to examine may be issued before issue joined, *ib.* 73; but special circumstances must be disclosed to warrant it, 2 N. Y. T. R. 259.

When a rule for a commission has been obtained, it suspends the cause until, on application to the Court, a *vacatur* is ordered and entered. But if the defendant appear and examine witnesses it is a waiver of his commission and the *vacatur* is unnecessary. *ib.* 73.

If the defendant has joined in a commission, the Court will not vacate the rule by which it was granted, on the application of the plaintiff, but will grant a rule to proceed to trial notwithstanding the commission, *ib.* 115. And where a defendant has obtained a rule for a commission, in which the plaintiff does not join, and a term has elapsed without any proceedings under it, the Court will permit to go to trial, *ib.* 503. So where a commission has been sent to England and eight months have elapsed without any return, the Court will give leave to proceed to trial; but this does not prevent cause being shown at the Circuit, why the trial should not then be put off, *ib.* or even if the usual time is not elapsed. 2 N. Y. T. R. 47.

In the case of *Juhel* v. *The United Insurance Company,* October 1801, the Supreme Court of New-York held, that three months was a sufficient time for executing and returning a commission arrived in London. At the January term 1803, of the same Court., it was decided, that where a plaintiff has delayed his own cause by a commission; and it does not appear that due diligence has been used, the defendant may apply for a rule for nonsuit, and compel the plaintiff to stipulate or be non-suited, as if no commission had issued. February 1804, a motion was made for leave to enter a judgment, as in case of nonsuit for not going on to trial. It appeared that a commission had been issued, but not that due diligence had been used in the execution of it, as eight months had elaped between suing it out and the sittings. The Court therefore said the motion should be granted, unless the plaintiff entered into stipulations. 1 N. Y. T. R. 527.

Where a defendant's commissioner has mislaid a commission, in consequence of which it is not arrived but is shortly expected, the Court will not grant a judgment as in case of non-suit, though there has been a former stipulation, but will allow to stipulate anew on payment of Costs. 2 N. Y. T. R. 47. After a second commission has issued, with leave to go to trial notwithstanding, the Court, under special circumstances, which have been discovered afterwards, will vacate the rule as to going to trial and allow a further time for the return. *ib.* 253.

A notice for judgment as in case of non-suit, is not waived by a notice for a commission. 3 N. Y. T. R. 140.

The act for the amendment of the law, of New York, 1 Rev. Laws 351. §. 11. does not specify that the commissioners should live in the State to which the commission is addressed, and the Court will therefore issue a commission to persons in that State to take the examination of persons in Pennsylvania. 3 N. Y. T. R. 105. *Tr.*]

TIT. 28. *Of the Warrant to be impetrated in rem where the debtor absconds, or is absent from the Realm.*

ALL that was written in the preceding Titles is to be understood as applicable to cases in which the defendant is actually arrested to respond in a civil cause. But if he has concealed himself or has absconded from the kingdom, so that he cannot be arrested, if he have any goods, merchandize, ship or vessel upon the sea, or within the ebb and flow of the sea and within the jurisdiction of the Lord High Admiral, a warrant is to be impetrated to this effect, viz: to attach such goods or such ship of D. the defendant, in whose hands soever they may be; and to cite the said D. specially as the owner, and all others who claim any right or title to them to be and appear on a certain day, to answer unto P, in a civil and maritime cause.

ADDITIONS TO TITLE 28.

[This proceeding is in nature of the process of foreign attachments under the custom of London, which has been introduced into most, if not all of the States with great advantage and success.

Its object is to compel the appearance of an absent or absconding debtor, and in case he does appear, to satisfy the debt out of his effects and credits. A respectable writer informs us that this process has gone into disuse in the Courts of Admiralty of England and Ireland. 2 Bro. Civ. & Adm. 435. The reason of it is that the jurisdiction of those Courts in instance causes has been so much narrowed by prohibitions that with the exception, suits for mariner's wages, certain cases of bottomry and salvage, and certain possessory suits for ships, all of which are, in most cases, proceedings *in rem*, there hardly remains to them any subject of civil jurisdiction. The process of attachment, therefore, has been disused, because there have been no occasions which would require a recourse to it. But if a case of debt should arise, clearly within the jurisdiction of a Court of Admiralty, as for instance, a maritime contract made at sea, to be executed at sea, which can indeed but very rarely, if ever happen; yet if such a contract should be made, and the debtor should conceal himself, or be out of the jurisdiction of the Court, there is no doubt but that the process of attachment would lay against him according to the course which is here prescribed by the authour. Huberus, *de jus in vocando,* says it is a remedy which is not warranted by the civil law, but the principle upon which it is founded, may be traced in the maxim of Justinian, *debitor, creditoris, est debitor creditori creditoris.—Tr.*]

" Sequestration, regularly speaking, is prohibited, yet goods may lawfully be attached in these cases :

1. If the defendant be suspected of flight; that is to say, if he does not possess sufficient real or personal property, otherwise not. *Scaccia. de jud. Lib.* 1. *c.* 35. *n.* 6.

2. If he be suspected of embezzlement; and he is said to be so suspected, if his shop remain shut contrary to custom: if at the time he play at unlawful games: if he borrow money upon usurious interest: if he do not possess real property equal to the debt: if he conceal his personal property in secret places, whence it can easily be removed; if he be involved in divers fidejussory securities: if he have played the like trick before: if hitherto he has been backward in paying his debts, and have at present, numerous creditors who are importunate. *Scacc. Lib.* 1. *c.* 38. n. 10. *Peck. de jure sistendi.* c. 16. n. 2.

This suspicion may be proved summarily and by half-proof; and sometimes by the oath of the creditor without any citation to the opposite party, according to the will of the Judge. *Scacc.* n. 28.

Before making the seizure, a full proof of the debt is to be made to the Judge according to his discretion, as *Scaccia* says, and a citation is issued to the party unless he be suspected of flight, in which case, the citation might be the cause of his absconding.[25] To the granting of the seques-

---

[[25] The original is to me obscure. The practice abroad is, to issue a citation before the attachment goes. If the debtor appear a summary hearing takes place; if he does not, the citation being returned is a proof of his absence or absconding.—*Tr.*]

tration any kind of proof, either by a publick instrument or instruments is sufficient. To discharge the sequestration, the debt is to be proved by such publick instrument or other writing as would be proof in other cases. *Scacc. n.* 24. &c.

But, according to *Peckius,* the proof may be made in another manner, because there is danger to be apprehended from the delay which might occur before the necessary proof could be obtained, and because an irreparable injury is not done to the debtor who may dissolve the attachment by entering bail. This other proof is according to the discretion of the Judge, who should have respect to persons and accurately examine the causes of suspicion.

3. If he be declared in contumacy, *Scacc. n.* 5. the Judges of our day, according to custom, decree a sequestration at the instance of the creditor alone, without the existence of any suspicion. *Scacc. n.* 11. If nothing is proved to the Judge and nothing is sworn by the creditor, the attachment is granted upon the simple assertion of the creditor. *Peck. nu.* 5.

Neither is it needful to execute summons or citations in such cases, elsewhere, but where the ship or *quarrelled goods* in question lie, or at the usual place of their haunting." Welw. Tit. 5. f. 61. [who quotes *De officio Admiralitatis Angliæ in fin. cum ibi citatis.*]

The debtor may be arrested either on or before the day he is suspected of flight; and so likewise may his goods be attached in order to compel him to put in bail or acknowledge his obligation, since in the mean time he might die or run away. But in other cases, the plaintiff is not only prevented from doing this by the exception, but he may also be officially hindered by the Judge, as soon as it appears to him that the time is not come.

I cannot reclaim any thing which I have loaned until the lapse of some time, because the borrower could have derived no benefit from it, except in case he be suspected of flight. It is not lawful for the creditor, of his own authority, to enter into the possession of the thing pledged until there has been some delay on the part of the borrower, to conform to the principal obligation on his part, unless there exists a suspicion of his being about to run away.

[26] A merchant became bankrupt and absconded; one creditor was prior, in point of time, to the others: he is to be preferred to the others, who are posterior and whose day had now gone by, if there is any danger in delay as to the prosecution of the pledge—nay he is to be preferred in the pledge. And although there should be no adjudication of the debt on that day or conditionally, yet still there is good cause to petition for security. *Peck. de jure sistendi. cap. 4. n. 6.*

The debt for which a person or thing was arrested was void; but the person arrested either

---

[26 The editor of this last edition has collected a quantity of matter in this note, marked [" "] which is wholly irrelevant to the subject of Admiralty practice, and which also is so difficult to be translated, that I should have omitted it entirely did I not feel myself pledged to give a translation of the fifth edition.—*Tr.*]

for some cause which existed before, or which arose afterwards, was bound to the person arresting : can this void arrest be justified by the subsequent cause of action? This question has its advocates on each side, and there are not a few expounders of the law of the highest authority who think that the arrest which is void in itself may be justified by the subsequent cause of action ; and *Soc. in tract. de citat.* says, if a person owed me a debt which became due on a certain day, and I, fearing that he would abscond before that day arrived, caused him to be arrested on a fictitious demand, in order that while it was in dispute, the day of payment of the real debt should arrive, for which he might be arrested, it is well; because those things which are null, not from defect of substance but of form, may afterwards, by the intervention of the true debt, be continued, and the party is not to be arrested anew. But *Baldus* maintains the contrary, on the ground that a case which has not a legal foundation cannot be supported by any subsequent event: and *Paulus. Paris.* at variance with himself, says, that in the first place the arrest is to be declared void and the person is to be restored to liberty; which being done you may afterwards begin anew according to law.

But *Peckius de jure sistendi.* cap. 17, says, if it manifestly appear that the arrest was not legally made, it is to be declared void, and the person at whose instance it was made is to be condemned to pay costs and damages : but, on account of the new debt which intervenes, the debtor is to be detained and not released.—

Therefore, he may be said to be liable to arrest, for the law does nothing in vain.

When a debtor is arrested for two causes and only one of them is proved, he is not to be released, nor is the creditor to be condemned in costs; for although in things which are indivisible, the useful is vitiated by the useless, yet it is not the case in those which are divisible and separable, although they may be in the same part or article. For debts are of different kinds, being not only divisible in their own nature but also in the estimation of the creditor; because he exacts them on different accounts; as on account of money lent and goods sold, things which have nothing common between them. The smaller sum is contained in the greater from the nature of the thing, because sums or quantities of money are divisible, not merely in the opinion of the person concerned. When he demands a greater sum, as for instance, £100 and £50 only are really due, he in plain terms, exacts the £100 *ex mutuo*, as so much due. Therefore there is no room to suppose that the £50 which are really due, are included in that demand. It is simply a debt which is demanded, and it is limited by £100; but the real debt is limited by £50, and so is not a part of the £100. The person who stipulates for £100 would not be content with £50. Therefore as he demands precisely that sum, he requires a definite amount which is greater than what is actually due. He will therefore be condemned in costs, damages and interest, *(interesse.)* The person sued will be acquitted, and the arrest be declared to have been unduly made. It is a different thing to demand more than is due in one action, from what it is to demand it in several actions: because with respect to each sum, he appears to institute a separate action, and so will be viewed as two different creditors, of whom one proves his claim and the other does not. With regard to the case which is proved, the person who was arrested is considered as a litigious person; indeed, in France, a defendant who is condemned to pay a smaller sum, than was demanded, is obliged to pay costs as a rash litigator, in not paying what he really owes. In the case which is not proved, the plaintiff will be condemned to pay the costs which the person arrested incurred by that suit: as he would not have been subjected to that expense, if he had not been compelled to prove the injustice of the claim: the reason of this is that in the latter case the defendant is successful.

He who could conduct his cause well but upon the whole does ill, does nothing: he who has done well in one part upon which the action can be sustained, although he may have failed in another part or cause is successful. It is sufficient that one of many causes which were suggested be true or good, as in sentence and appeal, where many things are necessary to complete an act, if one be wanting, the whole is vitiated; but to justify an arrest, the concurrence of many things is not necessary. But one cause being proved is, of itself sufficient. *Peck. de jure Sistend.* c. 47.

Tit. 29. *Of the execution of the aforesaid Warrant.*

The Marshal or other officer of the Judge, by virtue of the aforesaid Warrant must attach the goods wherever they may be, and keep them in safe and secure custody : and he must cite the defendant at the place where the goods are, and all others having or pretending to have any title or interest in them, by publick proclamation to those who are present, and also to those in whose possession the goods may be at the time of the attachment, that he doth peremptorily cite as well the said D. (the defendant in particular) as all others in general who have or pretend to have any title or interest in the goods which he has attached, to appear, each and every of them at the time and place specified in the said Warrant, to answer unto P. in a certain civil and maritime cause, as to justice shall seem meet.

Tit. 30. *Certificate of the execution of the Warrant for the attachment of the goods.*

The Marshal, or other officer by whom the above Warrant is executed, ought to certify it, with a copy of the schedule of the property annexed, and he should specify the time when, and the place where, it was executed, and that he cited the defendant according to the tenour of the Warrant. But if the mandatary be in remote places, then this execution is to be certified by an authentick certificate as above in Tit. 6. *of the certificate of the aforesaid Warrant.*

TIT. 31. *The exhibition or return of the said Warrant, and the Petition of the Proctor for the Plaintiff.*

I, N. exhibit my proxy for P. and I make myself a party to the same: and I exhibit the original mandate with the certificate indorsed, or, upon the truth of which certificate, O. the Marshal makes oath. And I accuse, of contumacy, D. the defendant, who was specially cited, and all others in general, who may have or pretend to have title or interest in the goods which have been attached, to appear here on this day, to answer the aforesaid P. in a certain civil and maritime cause. And I pray that they and each of them be declared contumacious; and in pain of their contumacy that they be decreed to have incurred the first default.* Publick proclama-

---

* Default, though it commonly signifies an offence in omitting that which we ought to do, yet here it is taken for a non-appearance in Court at a day assigned. *Cow. Interp. Verb.* Default. [vid. 1. Inst. 259. 1 Salk. 216. *Tr.*]

" Levatâ querelâ in Curiâ Admiralitatis, actore comparente et reo contuma citèr absente, omninò procedendum est ad defaltas et non ad sententiam definitivam, eo quòd non liquet de causà. Rought. in fine, in nig. Lib. Adm."

" If the party pursued be contumacious and will not appear to defend himself or his ship, or things challenged, the Judge, after three or four citations from the Admiralty, called *quatuor defaltæ* (for that called *unum pro omnibus* is not sufficient to convince one of contumacy,) especially in the claim or vindication of a ship, any part thereof or any other such like thing or goods, may proceed *ad primum decretum. Welw.* Tit 5. f. 60.

tion is then to be made three times, as well for those who were cited in particular as for those in general, and upon their failing to appear, they are to be pronounced in contumacy by the Judge, and in penalty thereof they are to be decreed to have incurred the first default, and the certificate of this decree is to be continued until the next Court day, or other day to be assigned by the Judge.

Tit. 32. *The manner of attaching goods or debts in the hands of others, to which the officer cannot have access.*

Sometimes the person, who, by loan or other maritime contract, is indebted to another, cannot be approached so as to be arrested; nor has he any property which the officer can attach. Yet you may be informed of persons in whose hands there are goods which belong to your debtor, or who may be indebted to him. In such a case you may obtain a Warrant similar to that which is mentioned in Tit. 28. *of other manner of proceeding*, &c. And the officer may go to the person in whose possession the goods are deposited, or who is indebted to your debtor, or which are liable or responsible to your debtor*, and attach

---

See Malines Lex Mercat. c. 18." [I believe this book is of no authority in questions of practice.—*Tr.*]

* For the debtor of a creditor is the debtor to the creditor of the creditor. *Sichard.* ad l. 3. Cod. de his quæ vi metûsve causâ, &c. n. 8. et ad l. 2. Cod. Quando Fiscus vel privatus. Where it is held that a sentence rendered against one who is indebted to me, if it be not paid, may be enforced against one who is indebted to

such goods or credits in his hands. He is to cite that person and all others to appear as before prescribed in Tit. 28. It is to be noted that in this Warrant the words, *the goods, debts, or sums of money belonging to a certain R. and being in the hands of the aforesaid person*, are to be included. These words are omitted in the case or warrant which was before mentioned.

TIT.º 33. *The certificate of the aforesaid Warrant against goods remaining in the possession of another.*

THIS Warrant is to be certified as the former one which was treated of in Tit. 6. and the persons who are cited, whether in general or in particular, are to be accused of contumacy and proceeded against in all things, as well as to the contumacy of the persons in particular as of those in general, according to the directions contained in Tit. 31. *of the exhibition or judicial introduction of the aforesaid Warrant, and of the Petition of the Proctor for the Plaintiff.*

TIT. 34. *Of the manner of proceeding upon the appearance of the person in whose hands the goods were attached.*

ALTHOUGH the person upon whom the attachment is served may not have any goods in his possession, yet he is bound to appear on the day

---

him. Et vide L. ult. Dig. Lib. 18. Tit. 3. De lege Commissorià.

assigned, and to allege that he had not any goods or debts belonging to D. at the time when the writ was served nor since, nor at the present time : and that it is not by means of any fraud nor collusion that there are none in his possession.

If he make oath upon the Holy Evangelists of the truth of his allegations, he is to be dismissed and all the acts of the plaintiff are to no purpose. But with this proviso, that if the plaintiff before the oath is administered,* be willing to allege and take upon himself the burthen of proving that the person has goods, or debts, &c. he is to be admitted to do so, and if he make out his proof, he should recover them with his costs. And note, that in this case the garnishee, in whose hands there appear to be goods or credits belonging to the defendant, is bound to respond to the plaintiff in this action, and to produce fidejussory security to all the effects mentioned in Tit. 12. *of the introduction of fidejussory caution by the defendant, and of the stipulations which are to be entered into by them.* And on the contrary, the plaintiff must give security as in Tit. 14. *of the production of security on the part of the plaintiff;* then a libel is to be given and in all things the proceedings are to be the same as in ordinary maritime causes which are instituted, directly for debt.

---

* For that being executed, *quere* whether it is lawful to prove the contrary ?

TIT. 35. *The granting of the second, third and fourth default.*

IN the cases which have been mentioned, the process is against the goods or debts attached; and when neither he whose goods are attached nor any other person appears, the proceeding is to be against them in pain of their contumacy as was prescribed in Tit. 30. *of the exhibition or judicial introduction of the aforesaid Warrant.* In the same manner as they are pronounced contumacious on the first day and in punishment thereof are declared to have incurred the first default; so, on the second day their contumacy is to be accused, and in punishment thereof, they are to be declared to have incurred the second default. Also the certificate is to be continued to the next Court day, or third or fourth Court-day, at the pleasure of the Judge. But on that Court-day, the proceeding and prayer are to be in the same manner as above, and he and the others are to be declared to have incurred the third default. The certificate is also to be continued to the above Court-day, and on that day the same course of praying, accusing and pronouncing is to be pursued and all who have been cited are to be declared to have incurred the fourth default.* The Proctor for

---

* Four defaults are to be pronounced against the defendant, if he do not appear within the term assigned to him by the Judge, before the Judge shall decree the plaintiff to be put in possession of the goods of the defendant, which is contrary to the ancient usage of the Court of Admiralty. Roughton *in fine* in Nig. Lib. Adm.

the plaintiff should then *ex superabundanti* accuse the contumacy of all the persons who have been cited as well in particular as in general ; and in pain of this contumacy should say, after this manner ;

" I give an article upon the first decree, and I allege, pray and do, &c. as is contained in the same ; and I pray that the same be admitted, that justice and right be done and administered, and that a decree pass in favour of my client, to put him in possession of the goods which have been attached according to the first decree."

The Judge shall then order proclamation to be three times made, for all the persons cited as aforesaid, as well those in general as those in particular. Upon their failing to appear, he shall pronounce them to be in contumacy and in pain thereof, he shall say, " We admit this article."

Then the plaintiff or his proctor, in support of the contents of the article, that is, in proof of the existence of the debt which he claims, ought to exhibit the letters obligatory or other instruments upon which the debt arose. And the principal party or sometimes the Proctor, according to information which he believes to be true, is obliged to make his corporal oath,* to be administered to him by the Judge of the truth of his claim. This being done, the Judge is accustomed to read the aforesaid article and say, " We pronounce and decree according to the prayer of the plaintiff."

---

* In debitis minoribus Vid. Tit. Prax. Ecc. 235, 236 per Ought.

Then the plaintiff or his Proctor shall give a bill of costs which the Judge shall tax: And upon oath being made by the Proctor, or the principal if he be present in Court of the disbursement of the sums as taxed, he may decree the goods or vessel attached to be appraised.— When the appraisement has been made according to the true value, and security has been given by the plaintiff to answer any one having interest in that behalf, that is, in the goods, provided he intervene for the same within a year, he is to be put into possession as far as the amount of his claim, if they be sufficient, otherwise as far as they may be sufficient.

ADDITIONS TO TITLE 35.

[The effect of the first decree, is only, in the first instance, to put the party in possession of the thing, and gives no power over the proceeds. All further proceedings of sale and power over the proceeds, must be by subsequent application to the Court; although upon such application a decree of sale and possession of the proceeds are almost matters of form and usually obtained as ordinary process of course. 2 Bro. Civ. & Adm. 403.—*Tr.*]

After the fourth default, the Judge should decree a mandate of execution, and he should issue his decree to the Marshal of the Court, directing him to put the plaintiff in possession of the goods of the defendant, wheresoever they may be found, to the extent of the debt claimed and declared for in Court, if they be sufficient, together with costs and damages. And if *bona mobilia* to such a value are not found by the Marshal, then to put him in possession of the *bona immobilia* to a sufficient amount, in order that the defendant being affected by the grievance, may be compelled to answer within the year and recover the possession of his goods, at first duly valued in the presence of the Marshal, and warranted upon this obligation in Court to be sufficient to abide the sentence and to pay the sum in which the party was condemned, and having given sufficient satisfaction for the expenses sustained on the part of the aforesaid party, *as Cod. 7. Tit. 72. de bonis authorit. Jud. poss.* &c. *auth. Et qui jurat. Collat. 5. Tit. 8. Novel. 53. de exhibendis et introducendis Reis cap. 4.* &c. *Decretal. Lib. 2. Tit. 6. de Litis non contest. c. 5. quoniam frequenter.* But if it is manifest, and the suit was not contested, the proceeding is at all times to sentence and not to defaults. *Roughton in fine.*

If he appear not before the time be fully expired, the Judge may proceed and adjudge the propriety of the ship to the plaintiff. *Welw. Tit. 5. f. 60.*

See Maline's Lex Merc. c. 18.

Tit. 36. *What things are contained in the aforesaid article upon the first decree.*

The plaintiff is bound to declare or relate in the aforesaid article, in what manner and upon what contract the debt which is claimed by him was become due: and in his conclusion, he must pray that right and·justice be done, and that he be put in possession of the goods which have been attached as far as they are sufficient to pay the debt which he claims.

TIT. 37. *Of the manner of proceeding if the person appear to whom the goods which have been attached belongs.*

As it often happens in civil actions, that a person is arrested who is not indebted to the plaintiff, so likewise may goods be attached when nothing is due. In such a case as soon as you are apprised of the attachment, it behoves you to appear, lest the course which is prescribed for obtaining a default should be adopted, and in pain of your contumacy, your adversary be put into possession of the property *ex primo decreto.*

If you introduce fidejussory security to all the effects which were mentioned in Tit. 12, *of the introduction of fidejussory security by the defendant*, the attachment is to be dissolved and the goods are to be delivered to you.

The plaintiff is obliged to put in security, file his libel, establish his claim and proceed, in the cause in all respects in the same manner, as if the cause had been originally instituted against the person of the debtor. Yet if you are pronounced in contumacy and have incurred any of the defaults, before you have intervened for your interest, it is necessary for you to pay all the expenses which have been incurred, before your goods are delivered, or you can be heard in the cause.*

TIT. 38. *Of the appearance of a third person to claim goods which have been attached as the property of another.*

IF your goods are attached as the property, or for the debt of another, and you intervene for your interest before the promulgation of the first decree; and yet nevertheless, the Judge shall have pronounced you to have incurred any of the defaults, the costs of these defaults must be paid before you can be heard, as in the preceding Title. This being done, your interest is to be propounded and alleged, and fidejussory security is to be given by you to abide the judgment, to pay the costs in case you fail in supporting your claim, and to ratify the acts of your Proctor. The plaintiff must also give fidejussory security to abide the decision, to pay the costs if you proceed, and to ratify the acts of his Proctor. During the litigation of the cause, the goods are kept under the arrest or sequestrated. And if you prove your interest they are to be delivered to you, and the plaintiff must pay the costs; and, *è contra*, if you fail they must be paid by you.

---

* The expenses of this sort of contumacy are uncertain, for if you be pronounced to have incurred one default, one sum is to be paid, and if you are in many defaults, it is to be increased according to the number of those defaults.

Tit. 39. *Of a third person intervening for his interest after the first decree.**

A third party intervening for his interest after the first decree has been pronounced, is not to be heard, as was said before in Tit. 37. unless the costs as then taxed be paid, and then the interest is to be propounded and alleged, and fidejussory security is to be given according to the effects which were mentioned in Tit. 38. of the appearance of a third person, &c. As the person who would have had the goods upon the first decree, introduces another fidejussory security at the time of pronouncing the first decree, as in the conclusion of Tit. 35. he is bound only to give security for his appearance from time to time, and at the hearing, to submit to the sentence, to pay the costs and to confirm the acts of his Proctor.

But in the same manner that the Proctor for either party is discharged from his office, and ceases to be the Proctor when the definitive sentence is pronounced, his office may also terminate as soon as he obtains the first decree, and the principal is put into possession of the goods, &c. Thus the person who intervenes for his interest in this way is obliged to summon the principal if he be alive, or his fidejussores who are bound for him, as above, to answer whatsoever, &c. as above in Tit. 35. to show cause why he should not be admitted to propound for his inter-

---

* De tertio interveniente Vid Gail. Lib. I. obs. 69. et Sequent. per totum. Peckius de jure sistendi. cap. 40. per totum et nu. 10.

est in certain goods which were lately taken under a first decree, as the goods of such a person; and he is to be admitted to defend his interest in this manner. If the persons who are cited do not appear, a Warrant is to issue for the attaching and arresting of them until they do appear. But if they have appeared, the third person ought to be admitted to prove his interest, and the proceedings are to be in all things, as in ordinary cases.

TIT. 40. *That the plaintiff may obtain a first decree, as well against the person to whom the goods which are attached are alleged to belong, as against all others who do not appear.*

ALTHOUGH a third person intervene for his interest in goods which have been attached by you, as the property of another who is in your debt, yet you may proceed and follow the aforesaid arrest, in the manner prescribed against your debtor, and against all others. And in pain of his contumacy and of those who are cited in general, excepting the person who has appeared, you may proceed to defaults and obtain a decree for putting you in possession of the goods, *quoad* those persons who have been declared in contumacy. But the goods are not to be delivered to you during the controversy between you and the third person who has intervened for his interest.

TIT. 41. *The manner of arresting your own goods when they are detained, occupied or possessed by another.**

It often happens, and especially in time of war or commotion, that your goods or vessel are taken by enemies or pirates, and afterwards brought to this kingdom; or are possessed or detained by others in some other manner; or the factor or agent of your correspondents in parts beyond seas, may consign certain goods to your use or benefit, and they are detained unjustly possessed by some person. In such cases you may obtain a Warrant to arrest the goods after this manner as your proper goods: and also a citation as well against those in particular thus occupying or detaining, as against all others in general, who have or pretend to have any interest in them, to answer you in a certain cause of a civil and maritime nature. Which Warrant being executed and returned as above, in Tit. 33, if no one appear, the proceedings are to be in all things as above, Tit. 31, and after the fourth default, the goods are to be adjudged to you; not for a debt as in the former case, but the decree is to be that in pain of the contumacy of those who have not appeared, the goods belong to you, and being your property, you are to be put in possession of them.

---

* Si bona fuerint in aliquâ navi vel intra jurisdictionem admiralli; imò et si sint in terram exportata, et in cellario imposita. Nam et personæ passunt capi in terrâ, in excambio vel alibi, et arrestari, et hoc fit quotidie. Vid. Brooke's Abridg. Tit. Admiral §. 1.

Additions to Title 41.

[This Title, and the two immediately following, are the only sections in this whole work, that relate to a proceeding which may be called properly and directly *in rem*, that is, a suit against goods or affects which the actor claims to be his property, or to be entitled to seize or possess by virtue of some lien express or implied; for the attachment of the goods of absent debtors, being intended for the purpose of compelling an appearance, may be considered as a suit *quasi in personam*. Here, then, clearly appears the falsity of the maxim which has so long prevailed in the Courts of Common Law, that the jurisdiction of the Court of Admiralty was merely *in rem*. It is to be lamented that the blind jealousy of those Courts with respect to this particular juridicature, has often carried them beyond the bounds of justice and even of truth. Vid. 3 Durn. & East. 348.

It is remarkable that no notice is taken in this title of vessels or goods taken by English subjects of their enemies. The fact is, that until the 44th year of Elizabeth, the prize jurisdiction was not vested in the High Court of Admiralty, but in a Board of Commissioners, called " The Commissioners for causes of depredations." But in this year, (1602) the Queen issued a proclamation for the purpose of repressing depredations upon the high seas, by the third article of which she ordained, " *that all admyrall causes, (except those depending before* the Commissioners for causes of depredation) *should be summarily heard by the Judge of the High Court of Admiralty,* without *admitting any unnecessary delay.* Rob. Collect. Marit. 26.

Such is the origin of the prize jurisdiction of the High Court of Admiralty of England. At the time when our authour wrote it was merely a Civil Court of Instance; and therefore we must not be astonished at not finding any mention of its powers or practice as a Court of Przie. It appears, however, that it took cognizance, incidentally, of matters which are now clearly within the jurisdiction of Admiralty Courts, as in the case which is mentioned in the text of English vessels taken by enemies, and afterwards brought into England. The property to these was often disputed on various grounds: such as their not having been brought *infra præsidia* of the captors, and other similar points, which from the old prohibition cases appear to have been, in former times, very much litigated in the Court of Ammiralty; and the Courts of Common Law showed a disposition, more than once, to prohibit its proceedings in cases of that description. Even so late as the 9th year of William III. Lord Holt and another Judge were of opinion that a prohibition should go to a suit by the original owner of a vessel taken by the French in time of war and carried into Bergen in Norway, in which the principal question was, whether she had been legally condemned. *Shermoulin* v. *Sands.* 1. Lord Raym. 271. At that time, such a suit was considered as within the jurisdiction of the *Instance,* and not of the Prize Court; for the appeal from the Court of Admiralty, in that case was carried to the Delegates, as in an ordinary suit, and not to the Lords of Appeal in Prize causes. Lord Raym. *ut supra.*

But in recent times, we find that cases precisely similar have been determined, not in the Instance, but in the Prize Court, and the appeals have been carried to the Lords of Appeal as in other cases of prize. *The Hendrick and Maria.* 4. *Rob.* 35. *Am. Ed.* 43. *Eng. Ed.* 6 *Rob.* 138. *Eng. Ed.* Same case, on appeal; and see Robinson's Reports, *passim.*

It is evident, from a passage in this title, that the Court of Admiralty, at the time when *Clerke* wrote this *Praxis*, had, or at least took, cognizance of bills of lading and freight. It is certain that in all their contests with the Courts of Common Law, they invariably claimed, among others, that particular branch of jurisdiction. But it was at length wrested from them, and they have been obliged to acquiesce. It does not seem, however, to have been disputed during the reign of Queen Elizabeth; for our authour appears to consider it as a part of the regular and well established jurisdiction of the Court.—*Tr.*]

TIT. 42. *The manner of proceeding in possessory and petitory actions.*[28]

If your goods have been arrested as the property of another, and you, either in pro-

---

[28 A *petitory* action at Civil Law, is a suit in which the right of property is in question: a *possessory* suit is that in which the right of possession only is contested.

per person or by another in your name and for your use, were in possession of them at the time of the arrest, you may appear in person before the Judge, or your Proctor may allege as follows:

"I exhibit my proxy literally for N. and I make myself a party to the same and to all in better right, &c.—moreover I allege to every effect in law, that at the time of the interposition of the arrest, my client was in peaceable and quiet possession of the goods attached not by force, concealment, threats, nor at the will of another. And therefore I pray that possession of these goods be decreed to my client in preference to all others, and that he be maintained in his possession; that the attachment which was interposed by others by the authority of the Court be dissolved, and that justice and right be done and administered."

If the plaintiff, at whose instance the attachment was made, denies these allegations, they are to be considered separately and conjointly, and a time is to be assigned for proving them.

Yet it is expedient that a protestation be made by you, that it is not your intention to proceed by petitory but by possessory title. And the plaintiff who hath attached the goods as his property, can allege himself to have been and to be the lawful possessor, and in the possession of these goods, and make his replication as follows:

Thus, an action of ejectment at Common Law, is within the latter description, while a suit of right is comprized within the former.—*Tr.*]

" That so far as the aforesaid N.* was at any time *de facto* in possession of the aforesaid goods, the same possession was obtained and is held by force, violence, threats, craft, fraud, or at the will of another."

And that allegation is to be proposed separately and conjointly; and the same being admitted on both sides, the proceeding is to be possessory, and upon proving the same, he shall obtain the possession of the goods attached, although the aforesaid allegations were put in generally, which mode is to be preferred. Yet it is lawful for the parties to specify and declare these general allegations according to the truth and fact of the case.

But this is to be noted, that before the party shall be put in actual possession of the aforesaid goods, they are to be appraised by order of the Judge, according to their true value, and upon proof of the appraisement, the party who obtained the possessory decree is to be bound in fidejussory security, to answer the adverse party in a petitory action—that is to say, he shall be bound to restore the aforesaid goods without waste, in case his adversary shall succeed in the petitory cause: and also to abide by the sentence, to pay the costs and to ratify the acts of his Proctor in that behalf: this, at least is to be done if his adversary shall have prayed proceedings in a petitory action, or shall have protested against proceeding in the same.

But allowing that the adversary is unwilling to proceed to the petitory action, on account of

---

* He who intervened for his interest.

the proof which was exhibited in the possessory action, because he who has succeeded in the former will probably succeed in the latter; yet, in further confirmation of his right in the aforesaid goods, the person who succeeded in the possessory action may proceed to a petitory action and obtain sentence *in petitorio*.[20] But he is bound to file a libel *de novo,* and if the witnesses who were produced in the possessory shall not support the right of the party in the petitory, he is at liberty to produce others. But if the complaint of the plaintiff was sufficiently established by the witnesses who were produced in the possessory action, and the proceedings in that cause are exhibited* in the petitory action they shall have full faith and credit. And the defendant may do all things, if not satisfied with the sentence in the possessory, he shall proceed

---

[[20] Formerly, and particularly at the time when this work was written, the Court of Admiralty of England had cognizance of petitory suits for ships when the right of property or ownership thereof was in controversy. See the case of the *Aurora* 3 Rob. 114 Am. Ed. By successive prohibitions it had been restricted to the enforcement of certain maritime liens, such as hypothecations and mariner's wages; but the Admiralty Court still entertains possessory suits for ships and vessels in certain cases, such as between part owners, 2 Bro. Civ. & Adm. Law. 406. And in some other cases, of which instances may be found in Robinson's Reports.

But in those cases the Court will not decide the question of property: and in passing a decree on the right of possession, it will look only to the clear legal title, without taking notice of any equitable claims which must be enforced in other Courts. The *Sisters* 5. Rob. Adm. Rep. 144. Am. Ed.—Tr.]

* For the records in one judgment are proof in another. Gail. Lib. 1. Obs. 103. in fine.

to his petitory action. And if he succeed in that cause, the aforesaid goods are to be adjudged to him and his adversary is to be condemned to pay the costs which have been incurred. In this petitory action the proceedings are to be in all things as in other maritime causes. And note, that the plaintiff,* before he is admitted to propound for his interest in the petitory action, is bound to give fidejussory security to prosecute his cause, to pay the costs, to ratify the acts of his Proctor, and to submit to the sentence. But although it is said above, that he who obtains judgment in the possessory action, is held to give fidejussory security for the restitution of the goods without injury; yet if they are in danger of perishing during the pendency of the petitory action, they ought to be valued according to the directions in the following Title.

Tit. 43. *Sequestration of the goods* pendente lite. *Vid. Cler. Prax. Eccl. Tit.* 189. *per Oughtonum.*

While the cause, whether it be petitory or possessory is in Court, the goods are to be sequestrated or kept under arrest, and delivered to the custody of some one who stands indifferent between the parties. But if the goods be such that they are liable to injury by being kept, or be otherwise deteriorated in value before the determination of the cause, the Judge, on the petition of one of the parties, although the

---

* He who first attached the goods.

other oppose it, if the premises be made apparent to him, may decree that the goods shall be valued by skilful and impartial men, named by the parties and approved by the Judge. The value of them is to be deposited with the Judge or his Registrar for the use of him who may succeed in the cause.

TIT. 44. *The arrest of goods by different creditors.*

IF any one be indebted to divers persons, and different Warrants are sued out against his property, and if the same be attached for the purpose of securing the payment of these debts; in this case, if the goods thus attached, be not sufficient for the payment of all the creditors, he is to be preferred who instituted the first action or procured the aforesaid goods to be attached, and he shall obtain the first decree of the Judge to put him in possession.

Also this same order and form is to be observed respecting the other creditors, if any property remain after the first creditor has been paid, although there be not sufficient to discharge all the claims.

TIT. 45. *Of the oath of calumny and what clauses are contained in it.*

OF the oath of calumny and what clauses are contained in it, read the title 151, in Clerke's Practice of the Ecclesiastical Court.

Additions to Title 45.

[The following is the oath here referred to:
You shall swear that you believe that the cause you move is just; that you will not deny any thing you believe is truth, when you are asked of it; that you will not (to your knowledge) use any false proof; that you will not out of fraud request any delay, so as to protract the suit: that you have not given, or promised any thing, neither will give, or promise any thing in order to obtain the victory, except to such persons to whom the laws do permit. So help, &c.

Or, thus, as an elder authour quaintly gives it in verse:

> You this shall swear that this your suit doth mean
>   Right just to be; at least in your esteem.
> That you, when ask'd, the truth will not deny;
>   Nor promise aught: neither that knowingly
>   You any false proofs will employ,
>   Nor urge delay, the cause to 'noy.

Clerke gives it in Monkish Latin verse, thus:

> Illud juretur, quod lis tibi justa videtur,
>   Et si quæretur, verum non inficietur,
> Nieu promittetur, nec falsa probatio detur,
>   Ut lis tardetur, dilatio nulla petetur.

This oath, says Clerke, in the title above cited, p. 213, is the *general* oath of calumny. It is to be taken once in the course of the suit, and generally immediately after the *contestatio litis*; that is, as soon as the cause is at issue; but, if it be then omitted, the Judge may require it at any subsequent stage of the proceedings. But there is also a *special* oath of calumny, otherwise called *malitiæ non committendæ,* which the Judge may administer to the parties and even compel them to take, either before or after contestation of suit, whether the *general* oath had been previously taken or not.

The oath of calumny has often afforded a subject of mirth to the practitioners of the Common Law, as being a useless ceremony and as often leading to perjury. But in an illiberal anxiety to detract from the merit of that excellent code, which has grown grey by *the awful hoar of innumerable ages,* its opponents seem to forget that many oaths analogous to this may be found in the Common Law itself. The *affidavit to hold to bail* is, so far, an oath of calumny: so is the affidavit which is usually made to postpone or continue a cause, that the testimony of an absent witness is material to the point in issue. An affidavit of defence, as it is called, which is made on a motion to open a judgment taken by default and in other cases, and which states that the defendant conceives he has a just and legal defence to the plaintiff's demand, is of the same nature. In Pennsylvania, the party who applies for a divorce, under an act of Assembly of that State, is obliged to make oath " that the facts contained in his or her petition are true, to the best of his or her knowledge and belief; that the complaint is not made out of levity, nor by collusion between the husband and wife, nor for the mere purpose of being freed and separated from each other, but in sincerity and truth, for the causes in the petition mentioned." 2. Laws Penn. 384. Dallas's Edition.—*Tr.*]

TIT. 46. *The proposing matter of defence, of propounding exceptions, and of corroborating the evidence of witnesses.*

ALL these matters respectively are treated at length in Oughton's Practice in the Ecclesiastical Courts. Tit. 99. 100. 101. 102. *of the manner of taking exceptions to witnesses, of propounding exceptions on the part of the plaintiff,* &c. *How often exceptions may be propounded in Ecclesiastical causes,* &c.

Yet note, that according to the ancient style and practice of the Court of Admiralty, exceptions of the same nature are admitted in general; a sufficient time being allowed by the Judge to specify these general exceptions, and for proving as well those in general as those in particular.

ADDITION TO TITLE 46.

[In the third edition this title concludes with the following explanatory remark:

That is to say, when general exceptions are admitted, if a probatory term be allowed for supporting them, and afterwards special exceptions are put in, a new term for proving them is not to be assigned, but the witnesses must be brought forward previous to the expiration of the term allowed for supporting the general exceptions.—*Tr.*]

TIT. 47. *The suppletory oath.*

THIS oath may be prayed and is granted in all maritime causes: but of the manner in which you must assign cause for obtaining it, read the title *of the suppletory oath of the principal* in the *Practice* Car. Ecc. per Oughtonum, Tit. 186. [a part of which I think proper to translate, and add to this chapter.—*Tr.*]

ADDITIONS TO TITLE 47.

[If the plaintiff has not fully proved his allegation, but has only given a half-proof thereof, (*semi-plena probatio,*) he may appear before the Judge and propound as follows:

" I, N. do allege that I have proved the alle-
" gations contained in my libel, &c. I say that
" I have proved them fully, or at least, half-fully;
" I refer myself to the acts of Court and to the
" law, and I therefore pray that the suppletory
" oath may be administered to me, for so the law
" and justice require."

Then the Proctor of the adverse party will say:

" I deny that those allegations are true. I
" protest of their nullity and I allege that the
" said oath ought not to be administered, refer-
" ring myself to law."

Then the Judge shall assign a time to hear the parties and decree thereon. And if he shall be satisfied, that the party who prays to have the oath administered to them, has made more than half-proof, or at least, half-proof of his allegation, he is bound to administer the oath to him in those cases in which the law permits it; consult, however, with experienced practitioners, as to what those cases are. Then the party shall make oath, "*that of his own certain knowledge the facts stated in his allegation are true.*"

If, however, the party against whom the oath is prayed, should be proved by his adversary, to be a person of infamous or bad character, the oath is then in no case to be administered to him. *Clerke ut sup cit.* 256.

As by the Civil Law, the testimony of one witness is not sufficient to constitute full proof of a fact, it is necessary sometimes in such and in other cases, when there would otherwise be manifest injustice, to complete the proof by the oath of the party. This is, what is called the suppletory oath. Thus, at Common Law, when a tradesman produces his books as evidence of a claim for goods sold and delivered, or work and labour done and performed, the books not being of themselves, sufficient legal evidence, the party is admitted to swear that they are his books of original entries, that the entries were made fairly, at the time, &c. and that the money which is charged is justly due to him. In this manner the proof becomes complete, and the oath which is administered to the tradesman, comes completely within the description of the *suppletory* oath. Indeed it is classed within it, in the civil law countries where tradesmen's debts are proved in the same way. Vid. *Ferriere Dict.* verbo *Serment.*

The administration of justice in different countries does not differ so much, as at first view it appears to do, for justice and right are nearly the same every where.—*Tr.*]

TIT. 48. *The exhibition of instruments in support of the allegations of the parties.*

OF the exhibition of instruments and the allegations that are necessary in that case, the manner of answering the same by Proctors and principal parties, of the form of setting them forth *pro confessis* when they refuse to answer, or do not answer fully, read Tit. 104. 105. 106. 72. 73. 74. 298. 299. concerning these matters in the *Prac. Ecc.* per *Oughtonum.*

But note these variations.

If the Proctor for the principal party refuse to take the oath to answer, or faithfully to dispose touching the libel or other matters propossed, to which by law he is bound to depose; the Judge may commit them to prison on account of this contempt, until they have taken the oath. Or he may warn them to take the oath by imposing some pecuniary fine, and if at length they still refuse, he may pronounce them to have incurred the penalty of the fine, and may order them to stand committed until the same be paid.

Tit. 49. *The comparison of letters.*

LIKEWISE of the form and manner of producing instruments of writing and of alleging, in order that they may be compared with the originals, and of the tenour of the report of those by whom the comparison shall be made, and of the exhibition of the same, and other matters which are necessary on this occasion, read Tit. 225. in the Prac. Ecc. per Oughtonum.

Tit. 50. *The exhibition of instruments of writing in the French, Italian, or German language, in support of the libel or other matter proposed.*

IF the instrument or other writing which is produced in proof of the allegation on one side, be written in any of the aforesaid languages, or in any foreign language, the Proctor by whom it is produced shall say:

" In support of the contents of the libel which has been filed in my behalf, I exhibit a certain instrument written in such a language;* and I pray that some one skilled in that language, and also in the English tongue, be appointed to make a faithful translation on oath, by such a day, and that he be admonished to exhibit as well the original as the translated copy on the same day."

---

* But whether the translation shall be taken without further evidence. Vid. Gomez. Resolut. tom. 2. Cap. 9. nu. 5. et Farinac. de testibus, Lib. 2. Tit. 6. quæst. 63. nu. 45. [I presume the translation would be deemed to be faithful until the contrary were shown.—*Tr.*]

Then the Judge shall swear some one who is good and true, and skilful in this matter, and shall admonish him according to the prayer.

TIT. 51. *The exhibition of the translation together with the original, and the petition of the Proctor who presents it.*

THE aforesaid original and the copy verified by the oath of the translator being introduced and exhibited, the Proctor shall say, *ex superabundanti* :

" I exhibit the aforesaid instrument originally written in the *Italian* language, together with a copy thereof translated into English; and I allege that all and singular the matters which are contained in the aforesaid instrument are true, and were treated, carried on and done, as is contained in the same, and that the copy which is exhibited is faithfully translated and agrees with the original."

This allegation is to be stated separately and the same being admitted, the Proctor who exhibited the instrument, shall make oath that he has faithfully propounded the instrument and allegation, and he may pray that the Proctor on the opposite side be put on his oath faithfully to answer the same. This oath the Proctor must take and he is bound to make oath, according to his belief, immediately, or at the next term if it be so prayed. And if the Proctor answer that he does not believe these allegations, a decree is to be prayed and passed, for the personal answers of the adverse party. This being done, the Proctor shall say:

" I pray that a copy of the translation of the instrument be registered, and upon this being done that the original be returned, and that the registered copy may have as full faith and credit as the original."

Then the Judge shall say, " We decree as is prayed." But the Proctor should take care that the original instrument remain with the Registrar, in order to enable his adversary or the Proctor of his adversary to make answer.

ADDITIONS TO TITLE 51.

[Instruments are for the most part two-fold, (scil) either publick or private.*

Publick instruments are those which are made by publick persons. And of these, there are many sorts: five of which are commonly observed:

1. An instrument drawn under the hand of a Notary Publick, or other publick person, either in or out of Court.
2. That which is sealed with some publick or authentick seal, (though written by a private) as of a Prince, City, University or College.
3. All writings whatsoever (though private) which are exemplified by the authority of the Judge or Magistrate.
4. All such writings as are taken out of publick registries, &c. or those made at the publick acts; [that is to say, *matters of record*.]
5. Those writings which are subscribed by the person and witnesses. And this is publick as to its effects.

---

* Wesemb. ff. T. de fide Inst. n. 2.

Private instruments are such as are made without any solemnity; and these are either
{
1. Accounts.

2. Private Inventories or Registers.

3. Private letters betwixt one friend and another, one tradesman and another.—*Tr.*]

TIT. 52. *The conclusion of the cause and the manner of giving information to the Judge before pronouncing the sentence, and the manner of pronouncing the same.*

OF these matters read the titles *de informationibus Judicia dandis, et de forma prolationis sententiæ in Causis Ecclesiasticis* Tit. 122. 127. 121. 114. 117. per Oughtonum, in which these things are specified and particularly treated.

TIT. 53. *Of an appeal from the definitive sentence.*

IT is lawful for either party to appeal from the definitive sentence or interlocutory decree, having the effect of a definitive sentence. It may be done either *vivâ voce* before the Judge or *apud acta* when he delivers the sentence or interlocutory decree, or before a notary and witnesses[30] within the fifteen days* which are allowed by the statutes of this kingdom for bringing appeals.

[[30] In the United States an appeal cannot regularly be interposed before a Notary. It has been so decided by the Supreme Court in the case of *Glass & Gibbs*, v. the *sloop Betsey*. 3 Dall. *in not.*—*Tr.*]

* Even within ten days; for the Stat. 24. Hen. VIII. cap. 12. speaks of appeals in Ecclesiastical causes only.

But of the manner and form of interposing these appeals, read the titles 289. 295. 274. 275. 290. 291. 294. 292. 293. 276. 277. *de appellationibus in causis Ecclesiasticis per Oughtonum.*

* Yet quere whether an appeal from a sentence in a possessory action will lie, because the effect of that sentence may be counteracted in a petitory action, or by the same Judge on an appeal from the sentence delivered in the petitory action.

Additions to Title 53.

[In England fifteen days are allowed to interpose an appeal, and the appeal must be entered within that time, Godolph. in Sea Laws, p. 208. This is by statute, for at civil law, ten days only are allowed. By the law of the United States, an appeal from the decree of a District Judge must be to the next Circuit Court, to be held in the same district. Vid. Judiciary Act, 24 Sept. 1789, §. 21. 1. L. U. S. 61. An appeal is given only from final decrees. As the appeal is expressly directed to be made to the next Circuit Court, a variety of questions may arise. It may be asked, can the appeal be entered at any time before the first day of the next Circuit Court, or must it be done within fifteen days af-

---

* On this question vid. Maraut. Spec. par. 6. act. 2. Et quandoque appellatur p. 305. Scacc. de Appell. q. 17. lin. 6. nu. 36. 37. 38.

ter the pronouncing of the decree as by statute in England, or ten days according to the rule of the Civil Law? Again, if the decree should be pronounced the very day before the first day of the sitting of the Circuit Court, a circumstance which often occurs, must the appeal be entered immediately, without any time being allowed for consultation and deliberation? *Quere.* In New York the appeal must be entered within ten days or the decree may be executed. *Reg. Cur.—Tr.*]

By the Judiciary Act above cited, §. 22. a writ of error, and not an appeal, lay from the decrees of the Circuit Courts in Admiralty causes; but by a subsequent law, passed the 3d of Mar. 1803, the former mode of proceeding by appeal is restored. 6 L. U. S. 315. The Act does not say that the appeal is to be brought to the next Supreme Court, nor within what time it is to be entered.

New evidence may be given in the appeal. *ib.* p. 316.

By the rules of the Civil Law also, new evidence may be adduced on an appeal, provided it be relevant to the matters which were alleged in the Court below; because on the appeal no allegations which are entirely new are to be admitted. *Per hanc divinam sanctionem decernimus, ut licentia quidem pateat in ex consultationibus tum appellanti quam adversæ parti novis etiam adsertionibus utendi ; vel exceptionibus* quæ non ad novum capitulum pertinent *sed ex illis oriuntur,* et illis *conjunctæ sunt, quæ apud anteriorem judicum noscuntur propositæ.* Cod. l. 7. Tit. 63. l. 4.*—Tr.*]

Tit. 54. *That it is not lawful to appeal from grievances, or an interlocutory decree not having the effect of a definitive sentence.*

ALTHOUGH you may file matter which is conclusive against your adversary, or take conclusive exceptions to his witnesses; or within the term you shall pray a commission to parties for the examination of witnesses or the like, and the Judge shall refuse to admit those things: yet it was always the practice,* not to allow an appeal from such grievances, nor from any interlocutory decree which has not the effect of a definitive sentence. Because relief may be had against such inconveniencies by an appeal from the definitive sentence; for in an appeal from such a sentence, it is lawful to allege whatever has not been before alleged, and to prove what has not before been proved.

Tit. 55. *What shall be called an irreparable grievance, and a decree waiving the effect of a definitive sentence, from which it is lawful to appeal.*†

IF any one arrest your goods as the property of himself or of another person, and you have appeared at the proper time before the Judge, and alleged your interest in the goods, and prayed to be admitted to interpose and prove

---

* This practice is more agreeable to the Civil Law as appears from Marantæ Part 6. Act. 2. et quandoque appellatur nu. 303.

† Vid. Marant. Spec. part 6. parte 3. verb. et demum fertur Sententia. n. 42.

your interest, and that justice and right be administered upon your case : Here, if the Judge tacitly reject your prayer, by proceedings contrary or prejudicial to your petition, as by proceeding to the first, second or third default, so that he may on the day of the fourth default adjudge your goods to be the property of another, or expressly decide against you, this is called *gravamen irreparabile*, and an interlocutory decree having the effect of a definitive sentence. Nor can you hope for any other sentence in that decree; and if, in such a case, you neglect to put in an appeal* your goods will be adjudged to another.[31]

So it is, if your creditor sue you for a debt, and in order to defeat his suit you allege that another action is pending against you for the same debt and before a competent tribunal; and the Judge either tacitly, by admitting *scilicet* the libel and proceeding in the cause, or expressly should reject your allegation, it is lawful to appeal as above. For these evils cannot be repaired in an appeal from a definitive sentence, nor can any other sentence upon such matters

---

* Vide tamen Sichard. in l. 2. Co. Ne ux. pro marit. in prin. where it is said that execution against the goods of another who was protested *de hoc*, is void.

[31 Brown, who takes Clerke for his guide in matters of Admiralty, here introduces a rule which deserves attention. He says, it is incumbent on the Procter, unless otherwise directed by his client, to appeal, either *apud acta*, or before a Notary *in scriptis:* for if he omits to appeal from a definitive sentence and any damage thence ensue, he is liable to an action by his client. 2. Bro. Civ. & Adm. Law. 437.—*Tr.*]

be expected. Read Tit. 123 *Quod sit decretum interlocutorium*, &c. *in causis Ecclesiasticis.*

Additions to Title 55.

[An appeal from grievances is interposed when witnesses are supposed to be admitted or rejected improperly. *Wesemb. parat.* ff. *de Appell. n.* 5.

An appeal from an interlocutory decree or from any thing but a final sentence, does not appear, as we have already observed, to be allowed from a Circuit Court to the Supreme Court of the United States. But, *quere*, will such an appeal lie from a District to a Circuit Court? In England where the appellate Courts are constantly sitting, there is but little inconvenience in allowing such appeals; but here, the Circuit Courts sit only twice in a year, and if appeals were to be brought from interlocutory, as well as final decrees, Admiralty suits would be without end. Perhaps there may be cases of *irreparabile gravamen*, where the District Courts would permit and the Circuit Courts receive an appeal, but they must necessarily be very few; no instance of the kind, I believe, has yet occurred.—*Tr.*]

Tit. 56. *Appeal from the Court of Admiralty.*

Inasmuch as it is lawful to appeal from the definitive sentence and the aforesaid interlocutory decree having the effect of a definitive sentence in the Court of Admiralty, to his Royal Majesty in his Court of Chancery, so from all definitive sentences, interlocutory decrees and grievances, by whatsoever inferior Civil Judges, or Vice-Admirals in the kingdom, it is lawful to appeal to the Honourable the Lord High Admiral of England, and that eminent man, the President of his Court of Admiralty, the Judge or Deputy whomsoever he may be of the same Court. For the Judge of this Court has jurisdiction over all causes of this sort.

ADDITIONS TO TITLE 56.

[By the Act of March 1803, appeals are allowed from the District to the Circuit Court, from all final judgments or decrees, where the matter in dispute exceeds the value of fifty dollars exclusive of costs.

In the same manner an appeal lies to the Supreme Court from any Circuit Court or from any District Court, sitting as a Circuit Court in cases of equity, of Admiralty and Maritime jurisdiction, and of prize or no prize. But the matter in dispute must exceed the value of two thousand dollars exclusive of costs. This value may be proved by affidavit.

In appeals to the Supreme Court, no new evidence can be received, except in Admiralty and prize causes; and such appeals are subject to the same rules, regulations and restrictions, as are prescribed in law in cases of writs of error.

But on error there can be no reversal in either Court for error committed in ruling any plea in abatement, other than a plea to the jurisdiction of the Court, or such plea to a petition or bill in equity, as is in the nature of a demurrer, or for any error in fact. Writs of error must be brought within five years after the decree which is complained of, is passed. But in cases of infants, *femes covert, non compotes* or imprisonment, they are allowed the same term after the disability is removed.

In appeals a citation must issue to the appellant, who is entitled to at least thirty days notice ; but this is not necessary if the appeal be prayed at the same term in which the decree was passed.* When the citation is necessary, it must accompany the writ or it will be dismissed.† But upon a suggestion that it was served, the Court will grant a certiorari. 3 Cranch 514. No appeal or writ of error lies in a criminal case.‡—*Tr.*]

TIT. 57. *Of the inhibition of the appeal.*

ON the interposition of the appeal, an inhibition is to be prayed from the Judge, before whom the appeal is lodged as in Ecclesiastical causes. Vid. *Cler. Prax.* Tit. 307. 303. 304. 301. 300. by Ought. Conset. Part V. §. 1. And

---
* 2 Cranch 349.
† *Ib.* 406.
‡ 3 Cranch 159.

that inhibition not only contains a command to the Judge, from whose decision the appeal is made, that he proceed no farther in the cause, and to the appellee in particular and all others in general, as in Ecclesiastical causes, but also an arrestation of the party appellee and a warrant or primary mandate in a civil cause to hold him to bail, until he shall appear to answer the appeal in the cause of appeal.

ADDITION TO TITLE 57.

[Writs of inhibition are not in use in the Courts of the United States. The Courts below take notice of the appeal, and of their own accord abstain from further proceedings, and the parties do the same. Yet it seems that it would be more regular to issue that process in all cases, as the party might otherwise be with difficulty brought into contempt, if he should proceed farther notwithstanding the appeal.—*Tr.*]

TIT. 58. *Form of the execution and certificate of the aforesaid inhibition.*

THIS writ of inhibition is directed to the party appellate, and to all other persons in general, as in Ecclesiastical causes. But the party appellate is to be arrested and detained in goal, unless he put in proper fidejussory security for his legal appearance, as in Tit. 4. *of the interposition of bail,* &c. and the inhibition is to be certified in like manner as an original warrant.

Tit. 59. *Of putting in fidejussory security in the appeal.*

If the plaintiff in the first instance shall appeal, he is not allowed to file a libel until he has put in fidejussory security to prosecute the cause, to pay the costs, to submit to the judgment and to confirm the acts of his Proctor. If the defendant in the first instance appeal, he is bound to put in fidejussory security to all the effects, to which *he*[32] was bailed in the first instance.* This, however is to be said, that although the defendant should appeal, if he should not succeed in the appeal, the cause is to be remanded to the Judge before whom it originated, with costs; which being paid, the other fidejussores who were bound on the part of the defendant *de judicato solvendo* are not released, but remain bound, in the same manner as if there had been no appeal. Why therefore should the defendant, as appellant, be bound to give new fidejussores *de judicato solvendo* in the appeal?

To objections of this sort, I answer, 1. There has been considerable dispute, whether the fidejussores who were put in in the first instance

---

[32 In the original, the word here used is, *Reus.* I apprehend that we should read *Actor*, as the appellant is the *actor* in the appeal.—*Tr.*]

* For the fidejussores in the principal cause are not bound in the appeal. l. penult. Dig. jud. solvi et gl. Marginist. ibid. Bartol. in l. citat. gl. in l. 2. Co de procurat. vide Fachin, Controvers. lib. 8. c. 57.

were not released by the sentence of the Judge, especially if that sentence was in favour of the defendant.

2. That sometimes it happens that the defendant has a just cause for litigating, because the Judge, in the first instance, condemned him to pay a greater sum than was really due. In such a case the sentence is reversed as to the excess, and the defendant is to be condemned in the real debt. In this instance the cause is not remitted to the Judge from whose decision the appeal was made. And therefore how can the plaintiff obtain the debt adjudged to him in the appeal, unless there are fidejussores in that appeal, who are bound *ad solutionem judicati?*

Also, let it be granted, that sometimes it happens, on account of new proof being introduced, or even upon that which has been adduced in the Court below, that the defendant upon his appeal is condemned to pay a greater sum than was adjudged in the sentence from which he appeals, and that that sentence, so far is retracted?

Whether in such a case, execution of the thing adjudged can be issued against the fidejussores in the first instance? Certainly not. Therefore, as it is said above, it was always the practice for the defendant upon his appealing, to give fidejussores *de judicato solvendo.**

---

* Vid. Scacc. de Appell. qu. 17. lim. 2. nu. 77. usque ad nu. 82.

Tit. 60. *The manner of proceeding in a cause of appeal.*

Of the manner and form of proceeding in appeals as to the propounding of a libel, the decree to transmit the process, of the privilege of the appellant to allege what he has not before alleged, to prove what he has not before proved, of the manner of justifying in the appeal from grievances, of the exhibition of the proceedings before the Judge from whose tribunal the appeal is made, and other proceedings in these cases, read the chapter in Ecclesiastical practice, in which these matters are specially treated. With this exception only, that the Ecclesiastical Judges, in punishing contumacy and contempt, employ the spiritual sword of excommunication against such persons as offend. But the civil Judges, whether in original causes or in appeals, resort to the secular punishments of imprisonment and fine.

Tit. 61. *Of the petition for a decree to show cause why sentence of execution ought not to be demanded.*

If the party against whom sentence was passed, shall have appealed at the time of delivering the sentence, and a term have been assigned for prosecuting the same, and a certificate of the prosecution of the same, and in the interim the Judge has not been prohibited from further proceedings, the Proctor who obtained the sentence ought to pray that the adverse party should be called upon to show cause why sentence of execution should not be ordered, and the costs be taxed. And this decree contains only a citation or nomination, and not an arrest.

But if no appeal was entered when the decree was passed, upon the expiration of the fifteen days which are allowed by the statutes for the interposing of the appeals, the aforesaid decree to show cause, &c. is to be prayed, as in Ecclesiastical causes.

TIT. 62. *Of the sentence of execution.*

IF the appellant, upon being cited extra-judicially to show cause why sentence of execution should not be ordered, should allege that he had entered his appeal at the proper time and place, as in Ecclesiastical causes, a term is to be assigned, at which he must prove that he has appealed. When that has elapsed, and there being no inhibition to the Judge, the sentence may be executed in the presence of the Proctor, who has alleged as before that an appeal has been entered. Likewise, if the appellant, at the time of delivering the decree, being cited, as before, to show cause, &c. upon his appearing, either in person or by proxy, shall not allege any cause why execution should not be ordered, it is to be ordered. But if he does not appear, it is to be ordered in pain of his contumacy, and he is to be proceeded against in all things as in Ecclesiastical causes. Tit. 130. 331. 131. per Oughtonum.

TIT. 63. *The decree against the principal party to pay the sum which has been adjudged with costs.*

AFTER the Judge, either in pain of contumacy, or upon the failure of the party to make his appearance, or in the presence of his Proctor in consequence of no cause having been assigned for which sentence of execution should not be ordered, shall have directed the sentence to be executed, a bill of costs is to be exhibited, which is to be taxed, and an oath upon that taxation is to be administered.

Then the Proctor shall say:

" I pray that monition issue to the principal party to pay as well the thing adjudged as the costs taxed within some competent time, and in case that it be not paid, that he be taken in custody and imprisoned until it is paid."

The Judge shall say:

" We decree as is prayed," appointing a certain time of payment, to wit, within twenty, thirty, or forty days, at his pleasure.

TIT. 64. *Decree or monition against the fidejussores to pay the thing adjudged, if the principal party abscond.*

THE aforesaid mandate being brought into Court with a certificate that the person has fled, or concealed himself, so that he cannot be admonished according to the tenour, the Proctor must pray as follows:

" I allege that D. the principal party has been sought for the purpose of admonishing him, according to the tenour of the mandate issued at my instance and that he is concealed, so that he cannot be admonished to pay the debt. Wherefore I pray that his fidejussores be admonished to pay, as well the principal sum as the costs, within some certain day, otherwise that they be taken in custody until the same is paid."

The Judge shall say, " We decree it," appointing a day as before in Tit. 63. Yet the Judge may, in the first instance, decree that the fidejussores be called, as before in Tit. 20, and he may decree that the principal party be called, to the aforesaid effect, by publick proclamation, as in Tit. 21. and if then the principal party do not appear nor satisfy the aforesaid mandate, the Judge may decree that the fidejussores be called as aforesaid, in the present title.

Tit. 65. *The decree against the fidejussores to pay the sum adjudged, without regard to the decree against the principal party.**

If the party, who is condemned, dwell without the kingdom, or has no certain habitation within it, so that he cannot be admonished to pay the sum adjudged, the Judge may, if he please, especially if the premises be proved to him on oath, or if the fact be notorious, as soon as may

---

* The fidejussores are bound notwithstanding the death of the principal. Vid. Pryn. in 4. Inst. Coke, p. 123, 124.

be after the time allowed for prosecuting and certifying has elapsed, decree that the fidejussores be summoned to show cause why the sentence of execution which is demanded should not be executed, without citing the principal party. So also, the Judge, after the sentence of execution shall have been demanded, and the bill of costs taxed, may, if he will, for the causes beforementioned, decree a monition against the fidejussores to pay the sum which is adjudged, omitting as above, the monition against the principal party.

Tit. 66. *Peremption* of suit.*

You may proceed in the same manner not withstanding an appeal[s] if it be not prosecuted within the term allowed by law, or if it be abandoned before the expiration of the term which was allowed by the Judge, from whose decision the appeal is made, although the appellant should have justifiable cause to appeal, as is noted in Tit. *de decreto dicendum causam,* &c. 321. *De modo procedendi cum appellans,* &c. 322. *De modo probandi appellationem esse desertam.* 324. *Cler. Prax. per Oughtonum.*

So of a civil cause, after it is instituted, if it

---

* L. properandum Cod. de judic. Authen. Ei qui Co. de tempor. et repar. appell.

[ss A suit at Civil Law is said to be perempted from the Latin word, *perimere,* to destroy, when it is not prosecuted within a certain time prescribed by law. It is analogous to a *non pros* at Common Law.]

be not finished and sentence given within three years, the instance is peremptory,* and no reason can be alleged or objected to impede the said peremptory instance. But the Judge, without respect to the justice of the cause, is bound to pronounce the instance to be peremptory.

TIT. 67. *The manner of proceeding in causes of contempt.*

IN the same manner as the Ecclesiastical Judge and the Ecclesiastical Jurisdiction, in executing process and other matters is contemned, so, very often, the civil Judge is contemned, not only in the execution of his mandates, but also by instituting actions before secular Judges, for matters relating to the jurisdiction of the Lord High Admiral and his Supreme Court of Admiralty of England. Ex. gr. If any one should institute an action in a secular case before the Mayor, or his deputies of the City of London, on account of a cause or matter which ought to be agitated and tried in the Court of Admiralty of England, and the cognizance of which belongs to the Lord High Admiral of England and his Supreme Court of Admiralty of England. The Proctor for the party injured is accustomed in those cases, to allege before the Judge of the Court of Admiralty, that a certain person, under colour of a maritime contract made and concluded without the kingdom, pre-

---

* And a sentence delivered after the peremptory instance is void. Marant. Par. 4. Distinct. 16. nu. 40. and Part. 5. nu. 58.

tending that his client was indebted to him in a certain sum of money, had caused him to be arrested in a secular Court: and to inform the Judge in a summary manner of the truth of this allegation, he exhibits a copy of the complaint, or, as it is called, the declaration, filed in the secular Court. And he prays the Judge to decree that the said plaintiff be attached, until he shall appear in the Court of Admiralty, to answer articles in a case of contempt, which it is usual for the Judge to grant upon an inspection of the declaration.

TIT. 68. *The appearance of the person who is attached in a case of contempt.*

IF the person who is arrested should appear, the Judge is accustomed *ex officio*, in order to avoid expense, publickly to exhibit to him a copy of the declaration, and to interrogate him whether the debt, which he claims, be founded upon a contract concluded in parts beyond the seas, or within the jurisdiction of the High Court of Admiralty of England.

And if he confess the fact, he is to be admonished forthwith to withdraw the aforesaid action. If he do this without delay, it is usual for the Judge not to consider him in contempt. But if he pertinaciously adhere to it and refuse to withdraw the action, although it is confessedly a cause of maritime jurisdiction, he is to be pronounced in contempt, and is to be committed to prison, and there detained until he withdraw the aforesaid action.

And he is also, for this contempt, not only condemned to pay the costs of the party grieved, but also he is mulcted in a pecuniary fine.

But at the time, if it do not appear from the declaration that the cause was instituted upon a maritime contract, which commonly happens, because in order to give jurisdiction to the secular Court, they are accustomed in these declarations to allege that the contract upon which the action is founded, was executed in a certain parish and war'd in the City of London, although the party who is represented as having made it never was in that City : or if the party who is attached, expressly deny that the action is founded upon any maritime contract, then he who procured the attachment is obliged to file articles or interrogations in a case of contempt, and to specify the place where, the time when, and the cause for which the said contract was formed. If he prove his allegations, he is to be allowed his costs, and the person who was attached is, as before, to be punished for his contempt.

But the process or manner of proceeding in these cases, is a summary proceeding, as in other maritime causes, and as they are accustomed to proceed in the Ecclesiastical Court.* It is to be noted that if the party proceed to justify the contempt *ut in § sed dato non constare*,[34] he is obliged to find fidejussores to submit to the judgment and pay the costs. Note, that the

---
* Vid. Cler. Prae. per Oughtonum, Tit. 30. 31. 33.

[34 I copy these words from the original, with a confession that I am utterly unable to explain them.]

Judge is not accustomed to decree a warrant for the contempt, unless, in the first place, the party who prays it, puts in sufficient fidejussores to answer the action in the Admiralty Court, if the party who is charged with the contempt, be willing to prosecute his action in the same Court. The like process or manner of proceeding is to be had against any other persons who contemn the jurisdiction of the Court of Admiralty; as, by the manner of executing the mandates of the Court, or by speaking scandalous words against the Judge or any officer of the Judge, on account of his executing a warrant.

PART III.

A FORMULARY

OF

LIBELS AND OTHER INSTRUMENTS

USED IN THE

ADMIRALTY PROCEEDINGS.

And know, my Son, that it is one of the most honourable, laudable and profitable things in our Law, to have the science of well pleading in actions reals and personals; and therefore I counsaile thee especially to imploy thy courage and care to learn this.
LITTLETON.

More jangling and questions grow upon the manner of pleading, and exceptions to forme, than upon the matter itselfe, and infinite causes are lost or delayed for want of pleading.
COKE.

PART III.

BRIEF DISCOURSE

SHOWING THE ORDER AND STRUCTURE OF A

LIBEL OR DECLARATION.*

Nihil dictum, quod non prius is a maxim, as true as it is general. So that to enlarge or say any thing in this discourse more than what others (of great learning and practice,) have said before, is a thing I aim not at; neither would I have any so far mistaken in me, as to think me guilty of so much vain glory and ostentation.—Neither were it possible for me (or any else, as I think) to reduce this discourse to a better method than *Wesembeck* † has done, whose words I shall insert, with some additions out of other authours, which will render this discourse so complete, as the meanest capacity (our insipid proctors, I mean of) may form a libel, without inspecting their precedent books; which they can no more be without, than a cripple without his crutches. I question not but the learned advo-

---

* Consetio's Practice of the Ecclesiastical Courts. *London*, 1708. [This essay, although it relate to the practice of the Ecclesiastical Court, is equally applicable to the Admiralty Courts.]
† Parat. ff. T. de edendo.

cates are so well stored with discourses of this nature, that this can be of little use to them.

1. *What a libel is.*
2. *How many and what are the parts of a libel.*
3. *How many sorts of libels.*
4. *What things are said to be proper to a libel.*
5. *What is the efficient cause of a libel.*
6. *The matter of a libel.*
7. *The form of a libel; deduced also from a syllogistical argument.*
8. *The next, and not the remote matter, ought to be expressed in a libel.*
9. *The end of a libel.*

A libel is said to be a diminutive, *a libro*, a book; whence formerly a paper was offered: in general it signifies every writing: figuratively the matter is put for the thing contained in it.—But properly in this argument, a libel is taken for the writing which contains the action :* Or a libel is nothing else but a fit conception of words, setting forth a specimen of the future sute.†According to *Lanfranc. (c. quoniam. de petition. n. 7.)* it is defined, the lawyer's argument.

2. It is said to consist of three parts. (*scil*) 1. the major proposition; which shows a just cause of the petition. 2. The narration, or the minor proposition. Whereby is inferred (in the species of the fact propounded) that there is cause just for the petition. 3. The conclusion or the conclusive petition, which conjoins both the prepo-

---

* Alciat. in prax. fol. 18. Speculator de libell. conf. sect. 1.

† Ummius disp. 6. th. 8. n. 38.

sitions, and includes the minor in the major.*
A libel therefore is a practical and judicial syllogism, as it were. Though *Speculator. de Libelli. confectione, Sect. quid Libellus, n.* 3 recites in parts somewhat otherways; for in the first place, he puts the cause of libel, which is the major proposition: in the second place, the obligation, which is the minor proposition; and in the third place, the action, which is the conclusion: For the petition itself is said to be the action: the conclusion consists in the petition, and not in the words related. And this is the chief part of the libel, which ought especially to be regarded in civil actions; not so in criminal actions or causes, because in them there needs no conclusion. By this the † plaintiff concludes, justly desiring from the premises and the things propounded, that the defendant may be condemned, both in the principal and the charges.‡

3. In respect of the subject-matter of the libels, there are only two sorts in use; the one of which is conventional or civil, (*à conveniendo*, from convening) the other criminal, (*à crimine seu querimonia*.) *In respect of its form, it is either simple (which absolves or declares the action, in a continued speech or oration as it

---

* Alciat. ubi supra Jason. Zasius & alii in prin. Inst. de Action.

† Alciat. ut supra.

‡ Speculator ubi supr. Sect. species. glos. in d. c 1. Lanfr. c. quoniam. ad verb. petition. de prob. n. 1. Alciat. in prax. fol. 103. Ummius disp. 6. th. 8. Rosbach, pros. tit. 33.

* Oldendor. p. de forma Lib.

were) or articulate, in which the merits of the cause are propounded by articles.

4. The properties of a libel, or those things which are said to be particularly proper to a libel, are these, *(scil.)* that it be round, (as the civilians term it) dilucid, concluding, not obscure uncertain, nor general or alternative.*

5. The efficient cause of a libel is the law, which deposeth a libel to be offered: But it commands principally that it be offered to the Judge (seeing his office is implored upon this petition) and then also to the adverse party.

6. As to what respects the matter of a libel: It is be offered in all causes, about which the judgment is stirred up, and a suit is commenced betwixt two: and that as well in civil as criminal causes, &c. but not always in summary causes, *(viz.)* in executions: for in these, any manner of petition is sufficient, though it be without writing: like as when it proceeded by way of inquisition, or where the office of Judge is implored in an extraordinary manner.

7. The form of a libel, (although it ought especially to be drawn, according to the style and custom of every court, yet there is no special custom extant,) ought to be drawn in writing; and in such manner, as that it may contain these five things, comprehended in these following verses.

*Quis, quid, coram quo, quo jure petatur et à quo,
Recte compositus quique Libellus habet.*†

---

* Ferrar. in forma Lib. contr. opp. lib. &c.
† Hortiensis de Libell. obla. Alciat. ubi sup. fol. 18.

Each plaintiff and defendant's name,
And eke the Judge who tryes the same;
The thing demanded, and the right whereby
You urge to have it granted instantly:
He doth a libel right and well compose,
Who forms the same, omitting none of those.

But the particular form of a libel* consists in the conclusion, which (what it ought to be) *Jason in sect. huic autem n. 13 Institut. de Action.* copiously disputes; so also *Myns. in Inst. de Action.* At this day, such respect is had to the conclusion, that it be sufficient to gather from its form, of what nature the action is, though no name be expressed: which seems to have been otherways formerly, at least by the law of *Codices.* To make this form the more dilucid and clear, we will dispose it into an argument or a syllogism, † *in Darii,* which shall in short comprehend the whole matter, and all the parts of a libel.

Every one who defames an honest man ought to be Ecclesiastically punished.
A. G. hath defamed a certain honest man, J. G.
Therefore the said A. G. ought to be Ecclesiastically punished.

8. Civil actions are either singular, general or universal, as was shown in the Practice. Those actions which are singular, are also either real personal, or mixt, as has been shown. Now in a real action, the next cause, and not the re-

---
* Ita formari debet ut ex narratis sufficiat jus agendi implicité resultare et in postea explicité in probationibus declarari. Wesemb. ubi s. n. 8. Anchor. cosil. 148. n. 6.

† Lanfr. c. quoniam. de prob. ad verb. petition n. 8.

mote, ought to be expressed,* as for example, I demand ten pounds of *Titius* which I lent him, and I desire he may be condemned to pay me that sum: here now the contract, or the lending money, is the next cause in a real action, and it is the remote cause in a personal action; for the obligation or bond arising from the contract, is the next or nearest cause in a personal action, and the remote cause in a real action: wherefore in a real action, if you say in your libel, I ask ten pounds of *Titius*, which he owes me upon bond; here your libel is so general, as it is in danger of being avoided, if the defendant excepts against it: but if in this action, you say in this manner, I ask ten pounds of *Titius* which I lent him, the libel is dilucid, by your making mention of the next cause: and so observe the quite contrary in a personal action.† But in a general or universal judgment or action, there is no need of mentioning any cause.

9. The end of the libel is, that it may propound the plaintiff's desire, and instruct the Judge and the adversary, as to the nature of the future sute, and to the foundation of judgment: for both the articles of the proofs are to be accommodated to the form of the libel, and the sentence is to be pronounced according to the same. Wherefore to the intent that the judgment be begun in due order, and be founded upon a certain thing, it is necessary that a libel be given by the plaintiff, though not admonish-

---

* Lanfr. ubi s. n. 3. Myns. Inst. de Act. in Rub. n. 15. et Sect. omnium autem. n. 14, 15.

† Lanf. ubi supra n. 3, 4, 5, 6.

ed thereto: the omission whereof doth vitiate the proceedings. Whence a libel is deservedly ranked among the substantial proceedings: for no libel existing, the proceedings are rendered null, &c.

10. Agreeable to what has been said, I will here obviate the form of a libel, as it is offered before the Judge of the Ecclesiastical Courts. And in the first place, it must be drawn in the name and style of the Judge, as *Alciatus* has also observed in his form, set down in his practice, at fol. 18. (*viz.*)

> In the name of God amen. *Before you the worshipful* H. W. *Doctor of Laws, principal official of the beautiful consistory court of* York, &c. *The party of* J. G. *against* A. G. &c. *allegeth and complaineth, and propoundeth,* &c.

Imprimis, He doth propound and article, that the said *J. G.* was and is a man very honest, just and upright, of good fame, life and honest conversation, aspersed, defamed, with no crime (at least such as is notorious) except such as is afterwards mentioned, and is commonly reputed, had, named and esteemed as such, &c.

Item, That notwithstanding the premises, the said *A. G.* out of a malign spirit, in the months of *A. M. I.* &c. in this present year, 1630, in in one or other of the said months, within the said parish* of *D.* aforesaid, or some other

---

* Ratio hujus apud Myns. Inst. de Action. Sect. Malef. et Sect. curare autem.

place within the said parish, maliciously and out of an intent of defaming and injuring the said *J. G.* hath defamed and injured him, and hath said, uttered, &c. some reproachful and defamatory words, of and against the said *J. G.* and especially these words following, or the like in effect, (*viz.*) the said *A. G.* said and reported (though falsely,) diverse and sundry times, or at least once, speaking to the said *J. G. thou hast got a wench with child,* &c. The party doth propound and article, as to such a time and manner of speaking the words, &c.

Wherefore proof being made upon the premises, the party of the said *J. G.* doth request or petition, that the said *A. G.* for such excessive rashness in the premises, and concerning the same, may be corrected and punished according to your pleasure; and also that he may be condemned in charges, made and to be made in this cause, on the behalf of the said *J. G. &c.*

Mynsinger in Inst. de injuriis Sect. in summa, concludes thus. Wherefore the plaintiff desires that (in order to repair his fame and good name) the defendant aforenamed, may be compelled by you, and your definitive sentence, to disown, confess and declare publicly, that the said defamatory and injurious words, were unadvisedly and against the truth, spoke and uttered by him, &c. or otherways, that right and justice be administered, &c.

No. 1.

*Summons of a Judge or Justice of the Peace to the Master, to answer a claim for wages.**

TO A. B. MASTER OF THE SHIP FAME.

You are hereby required to attend at my office, No.—— —— Street, in the City of Baltimore, on Monday next, the —— day of —— at —— o'clock in the forenoon, to show cause why process of attachment should not issue against the said ship Fame, whereof you are Master, her tackle, apparel and furniture, according to the rules of Admiralty Courts, to answer the claims of Thomas Tackle for services as a Mariner on board the said ship during her voyage from the port of —— to the port of —— which voyage ended on the —— day of ——.

Given under my hand, this —— day of—— in the year aforesaid.   T. G.

        one of the Justices of the Peace for Baltimore County.

No. 2.

Certificate of the Magistrate to the Clerk of the District Court.

I do hereby certify, that there appears to me sufficient cause of complaint whereon to found

---

* *Vide* p. 7. *ante.*

Admiralty process against the ship Fame, her tackle, apparel and furniture, to answer the complaint of A. B. late a Mariner on board the said ship.

No. 3.

Libel for Seamen's Wages.

To the Honourable *James Winchester*, Judge of the District Court of the United States, for Maryland District,

The Libel of Thomas Bowling, Mariner, humbly showeth:

THAT your Libellant, on the tenth day of June in the year of our Lord one thousand eight hundred and four at the Port of Baltimore in the said District, at the request of Daniel Jones, Master of the ship Henrietta, then lying at anchor in the said Port, shipped as a Mariner on board said ship, to perform a voyage on the *high seas* and within the jurisdiction of this Honourable Court, to wit, from the said Port of Baltimore to Liverpool, thence to any other port in Great Britain, and thence back to the said Port of Baltimore, at the wages of twenty dollars per month, as will more fully appear by the shipping articles signed by your Libellant, in which his contract for the said voyage is fully set forth, and which he prays may be produced by the said Daniel Jones to this Honourable Court.

And your Libellant further showeth, that he proceeded on the said voyage in the said ship to the said port of Liverpool, whence he proceeded to the port of London and thence back to the Port of Baltimore aforesaid, at all times and in all things doing his duty faithfully as a Mariner on board the said ship. And your Libellant further showeth, that the said ship arrived at the said Port of Baltimore on the ―― day of ―― in the year of our Lord one thousand eight hundred and ――, where she was safely moored and her cargo safely landed, and your Libellant was discharged from the said ship without being paid the wages so by him earned as aforesaid or any part thereof, except what is duly credited in the schedule hereunto annexed; and there is now due unto your said Libellant, by reason of his said services, the sum of ―― dollars, which the said Daniel Jones hitherto hath altogether refused and still doth refuse to pay, although often thereto required by your Libellant.

[* Your Libellant further showeth, that the said ship is about to proceed to sea before the end of ten days next after the delivery of her cargo; and unless your Libellant can obtain immediate process he may not be able to enforce the payment of his aforesaid wages by the decree of this Honourable Court.]

To the end therefore that your Libellant may

---

* This allegation is necessary when, the vessel being about to proceed to sea before the expiration of ten days from the delivery of her cargo, the seaman requires immediate process, without the delay of a summons—*Vid.* 1. *L. U. S.* p. 134. § 6.

obtain relief in the premises, he prayeth process of attachment against the said ship Henrietta, her tackle, apparel and furniture, according to the course of Admiralty Courts, and monition as is usual in like cases generally and in special to the said Daniel Jones, that he may on his corporal oath, true and proper answers make to this Libel and to the interrogatories hereunto annexed. And your Libellant prays that the said ship Henrietta, her tackle, apparel and furniture may be condemned and sold to pay the wages due as aforesaid to your Libellant, and that he may have such further relief in the premises as to justice shall seem meet.

☞ The Proctor will annex such interrogatories as may suit his case, and a statement upon oath, of the Libellant's, claim, in the form of an account against the vessel.

No. 4.

*Attachment against the Vessel.**

THE UNITED STATES OF AMERICA:

MARYLAND DISTRICT, ss.

To the Marshal for Maryland District, Greeting:

WE command you, that you attach, seize, take, and safely keep the —(A. B. master of the ——) *her tackle, apparel and furniture, commanded by* ——, *and now lying at the Port of*

---

* The Attachment against the person is similar to the above, excepting, that the words printed in *italicks* are omitted, and those included in a parenthesis are inserted.

Baltimore, to answer the libel of ⸺, and how you shall execute this precept you make known to us in our District Court for the District aforesaid, at the Court-house in the City of Baltimore, ⸺, and have you then and there this writ.— Witness the Honourable James Winchester, Esq. Judge of our said District Court, this ⸺ day of ⸺ 180

Clk. Dist. Court Maryland.

No. 5.

*Monition against the Vessel.**

THE UNITED STATES OF AMERICA:

MARYLAND DISTRICT SS.

To the Marshal for Maryland District Greeting:

WHEREAS ⸺ ha ⸺ exhibited ⸺ Libel or Complaint in the District Court of the United States for Maryland District, stating, alleging and propounding, that [*here recite the purport of the Libel.*]

And whereas the Judge of the District Court for the District aforesaid, hath ordered and directed ⸺ next, *for all persons concerned* (the said ⸺) to be cited and intimated to appear in the Court-house in the City of Baltimore, and show cause, if any *they have*, (he hath) why

---

* In the Monition against the person the above form is used, with this difference, that the words printed in *italicks* are omitted, and those which immediately follow them, included in a parenthesis, are inserted.

judgment should not pass as prayed:—You are therefore hereby authorised, empowered and strictly enjoined, peremptorily to CITE and ADMONISH ——— *persons whatsoever, having or pretending to have any right, title, interest or claim in or to the said* ——— (the said ———) libelled against as aforesaid, by *publickly affixing* (shewing) this monition *on the Main-Mast of the said* ——— (to the said ———) *for some time, and by leaving there affixed* (and leaving with him) a true copy thereof: and by all other lawful ways, means and methods whatsoever, whereby this MONITION may be made most publick and notorious, to be and appear at the time and place aforesaid, before the Judge aforesaid: and also to attend upon every session and sessions to be held there and from thence, until a DEFINITIVE sentence shall be read and promulged in the said business inclusively, if *any of them* (he) shall shall think it *their* (his) duty so to do; to hear, abide by and perform all and singular such judicial acts as are necessary and by law required to be done and expedited in the premises; and further to do and receive what unto law and justice shall appertain, under the pain of the law and contempt thereof, the absence and contumacy of *them* (him) *and every of them in any wise notwithstanding.*—And whatsoever you shall do in the premises, you shall duly certify unto the Judge aforesaid, at the time and place aforesaid, together with these presents.

    Witness, the Honourable James Winchester, Judge of our said District Court, this ——— day of ——— in the year of our Lord ———

Libel for Materials furnished to a Vessel.

TO THE HONOURABLE, &c.

The Libel of T— F— and J— K—, Merchants, trading jointly by the name of F— and K—, humbly showeth:

THAT your Libellants, at sundry times, between the fourth day of December in the year of our Lord eighteen hundred and seven, until the twenty-seventh day of June in the year eighteen hundred and nine, at the special instance and request of J— S— and W— B. S— who were employed in building a new brig or vessel in Nanticoke River in the said District, did provide, furnish and deliver to the use of the said brig, certain rudder and irons, spikes, cordage and other materials necessary in the building and rigging of the said brig, and for her safety and navigation on the high Seas; which materials and the cost of them are particularly set forth and described in the Account or Schedule hereunto annexed, and amount to the sum of three hundred and seventy-one dollars and nineteen cents, current money.

Your Libellants further show, That although the said brig is not yet completely finished, and hath not, to their knowledge, received any name whereby to distinguish her, the owners are about to send her out of this District, without paying your Libellants for the materials furnished by them as aforesaid, and which have been applied upon the said brig; and your Libellants have not accepted any other security for their said claim than their *lien* on the said brig, which they have not in any manner consented to release.

To the end therefore that by the decree of this Honourable Court, your Libellants may obtain relief in the premises, they pray process of attachment against the said new brig, now lying at Vienna in Nanticoke River, her tackle, apparel and furniture, according to the custom of Admiralty Courts, and MONITION as is usual in like cases, generally, and in special to the said J— S— and W— B. S—, that they may, on their corporal oaths, true, full and perfect answer make to this Libel, and all the matters herein set forth, and may disclose and declare whether any and what name has been given to the said brig, so that the same may be inserted in and made a part of this Libel. And your Libellants pray that by the Decree of this Honourable Court, the said brig may be condemned and sold for the payment of the claim of your Libellants, and that they may have such further and other relief as the nature of their case may require, and they will pray, &c.

Libel in a Case of Damage.

TO THE HONOURABLE, &c.

THE Libel of *I. P.* owner of the brig called the *Constitution* against the ship called the *Perseverance*, whereof *T. J.* now is or lately was master, her tackle, apparel and furniture, humbly showeth:

That in the month of ——— in the year of our Lord ——— the said brig *Constitution*, whereof your Libellant was master, was at the Port of Baltimore, and designed on a voyage thence to the port of London with a valuable cargo on board and was at that time, and at the time of the damage hereinafter plead, a tight, staunch and well built vessel, of the burthen of eighty tons or thereabouts, and was completely rigged and well and sufficiently found and furnished with tackle, apparel and furniture, and had on board and in her service the said *J. P.* and four mariners, which were and are a full and sufficient complement or number of hands to take care of and navigate the said brig or any other vessel of the like burthen and rigging, on the like service.

That on or about the ——— day of ——— in the year aforesaid, the said brig *Constitution* with the said *J. P.* as master and her aforesaid crew or complement of hands on board, found, provided and furnished as aforesaid, and loaded with a valuable cargo as aforesaid, sailed from the Port of Baltimore on her aforesaid voyage: that on the following day your Libellant being then upon the deck of his said brig *Constitution*, and the said brig being upon her starboard tack, with the wind all South-west or thereabouts, under close reefed top-sail, upon the high seas, within the flux and reflux thereof, and within the jurisdiction of this Honourable Court, discovered the ship *Perseverance* whereof the said *T. J.* then was master coming or her larboard tack, right for the said brig *Constitution*; whereupon your libellant and his crew hailed the said ship *Perse-*

verance and begged the master and people on board of the said ship *Perseverance* to bear up or they would certainly run on board: yet the master and crew of the said ship *Perseverance* although they heard your Libellant and his crew calling to them and cautioning them to bear up as aforesaid, either from malicious obstinacy or want of skill or power, refused or neglected so to do.

That there being no other means of preventing damage but by putting both the said vessels about on the other tack, the people on board the said brig *Constitution* put their said brig about on the other tack accordingly, and your Libellant doth expressly allege that if the people on board the said ship *Perseverance* had done the like no damage whatever would have happened; but instead of so doing, the people on board the said ship *Perseverance* did not so much as shiver or back one sail, but come with all the force the wind and her sails could give her against the said brig *Constitution*, struck her on the larboard quarter of her stern, broke her stern post, upset her quarter-deck, broke several planks on her larboard quarter, and did her other considerable damage, and thereupon some of the Mariners on board the said brig *Constitution* conceiving her to be sinking from the violence of the blow took to the boat to save their lives, and notwithstanding the same was observed by the people on board the said ship *Perseverance*, they sailed away from and left the said brig *Constitution*, without affording the least assistance to her or her crew.

That after the said brig *Constitution* was so struck and received the damage aforesaid, your Libellant did every thing that an able and experienced Mariner could do for the preservation of his said brig and her cargo; but finding, notwithstanding the pumps were kept working, and every exertion was made to stop her leaks, that she was in a sinking condition; he, your Libellant, to prevent the said brig and cargo from being totally lost, determined to and did run the said brig on shore near Cape Fear, with all possible care and diligence.

Wherefore your Libellant prays, &c.

☞ This Libel is abridged from one which is inserted in Judge Marriot's *formulare*. The case is undoubtedly within the jurisdiction of Admiralty, in England, but I understand that a contrary doctrine has been held in Pennsylvania by Judge Peters, who dismissed a libel. My information, however, is not positive. By the Laws of Oleron art. 14. and the ordinance of Wisbuy art. 26. 50. 67. and 70. each ship must bear a moiety of the damage if the injury was accidental. But if the party running against the other do not swear that he did not do it designedly, he must pay the whole loss.

In England, Sir James Marriott says, that, when the Judge has any doubts in regard to the manner of navigating ships course, position and situation, he calls for the assistance of two masters of the Trinity House, to explain. In our Courts I presume that experienced masters would be summoned, as witnesses, for this purpose.

Salvage.

To the Honourable *Richard Peters*, Esq. Judge of the District Court of the United States, in and for the Pennsylvania District:

The libel of *J. W.* owners of the ship *Amiable* and *W. P.* Captain of the said ship, for themselves and all others entitled, humbly showeth:

That on Saturday the 10*th* day of Nov. inst. about 7 o'clock in the morning, the said *W. P.* being on a voyage in the said ship from Charleston, in South-Carolina to Philadelphia, he discovered a ship in distress, upon which he shortened sail, hauled up for her, and found her to be a ship *La Bella Creolle* of Bordeaux, commanded by — Denney, bound for P. au P. to b. That the Captain declared that they were in great distress the ship being sinking under them and entreated the said *W. P.* to stay by them, to which the said *W. P.* agreed, and the wind then blowing very fresh, the said *W. P.* made light sail in order to continue in their company—that the people on board the said *La Belle Creolle* not understanding his intentions appeared alarmed and renewed their signals of distress, upon which the said *W. P.* wore ship and ran under their stern, when they again besought him not to leave them as their ship would undoubtedly founder; upon which the said *W. P.* assured them that he would stay by them and relieve them as soon as the weather moderated—that the next day about 11 o'clock he sent his yawl with his mate and four hands on board the said ship *La Belle Creolle*, who assisted to pump out the said ship, and to bend the fore top-sail; that the said mate on his return reported that the said ship was old and rotten, and in a very bad situation, and in his opinion unfit to proceed on her voyage, whereupon the mate by the orders of the said captain *P*. returned to the said ship with assurances that he the said captain *P*. would stay by them until the next day, upon which the said captain *D*. wrote a note to the said captain *P*. requesting him to stay by them and endeavour to bring them into some Port, and that he should be allowed whatever the Law would give, to which the said captain *P*. agreed—that the said ships continued in company during the rest of the day, and during the rest of the night, continued to make signals of distress and so continued during the ensuing day the 12*th* inst. That the said captain *D*. on the 12*th* inst. being hard blowing weather, threw overboard part of his cargo; that on the 13*th* inst. the weather moderated in some degree when the said *P*. run down and on consultation with the said captain *D*. sent his boat on board to lighten the ship and to take her in tow—the boat returned with a few bags of Coffee, in which boat the said captain *D*. came on board the *Amiable*, to propose that the said vessel should be taken in tow when the weather moderated—that it continued to blow fresh that night and the 14*th*. The said captain *D*. continued to make signals of distress, but on the 15*th* the weather moderated, and at half past 3. P. M. the said captain *D*. hoisted colours half mast high, upon which the said captain *P*. bore down to them when they declared their ship was sinking and begged to be taken out—that he ordered them to hoist out their boat and put provision into her and fall to leward and he would bear down and take them in—that it again began to blow fresh with a heavy sea, and as they were hoisting out their boat she dropped in pieces, whereupon they begged the said *P.* to send his boat to their assistance; that the said *P.* called together his officers and crew to enquire which of them would undertake in the high wind and heavy sea which then prevailed to go and bring away the crew; that his two mates, and two of the seamen agreed to go and got out the boat, that with considerable pains and danger bringing provisions and two men at a time they removed the captain and his whole crew consisting of twenty three men and one passenger; that previous to leaving the said ship, the crew proposed to set her on fire, to which however, the said captain *P.* upon being informed of the proposal objected, and the said captain *D.* and his crew being on board the *Amiable,* declared that they relinquished and abandoned the said ship *La Belle Creolle* and every thing on board her—that the next morning being the 16*th,* the said captain *P.* hoisted out the yawl and in the course of the day took out of the said ship as much of the cargo as possible amounting as your Libellants believe to be about twenty thousand wt. of Coffee, four or five barrels a few kegs of Sugar, twelve or thirteen bales of Cotton, and about twenty-three bags of Indigo, &c. &c. &c. *(specifying the Articles saved;)* that night coming on, the ship sinking fast, and there appearing no chance of preserving her, at the renewed request of the said captain *D.* and to prevent her injuring other vessels, they set fire to the said ship and left her, and the said captain *P.* with the said captain *D.* and his crew and passengers aforesaid arrived in the Port of *P.* the 19*th* of November inst.

Now inasmuch as the said *W. P.* hath with so much difficulty and danger saved from the said ship *La Belle Creolle* the Articles aforesaid, which would otherwise in all human probability have been totally lost; may it please your honour to order the said articles being now on board the said ship *Amiable* to be attached and taken by the process of this honourable Court, and that a MONITION issue to all persons concerned to show cause, if any they have, why a reasonable Salvage should not be decreed thereout to the Libellants and all others intitled, and that such further and other steps shall be taken as the course of this honourable Court shall require.

J. W.
W. P.

W. RAWLE, *Attorney for Libellants.*

To the honourable JOHN SLOSS HOBART, *esquire, Judge of the District Court of the United States for the New York District.*

The libel of Silas Talbot esquire commander of the United States ship of war the *Constitution* on behalf as well of the United States as of himself and the officers and crew of the said ship, against the ship *Amelia,* her tackle, apparel, furniture and cargo:

The said Libellant for and on behalf as aforesaid, doth hereby propound, allege and declare to this honourable court, as followeth (to wit)

First, That pursuant to instructions for that purpose from the President of the United States this Libellant in and with the said United States ship of war the *Constitution* and her officers and crew, did subdue, seize and take upon the high seas, the said ship or vessel called the *Amelia* of the burthen of about 370 tons, with her apparel, guns, and appurtenances, and a valuable cargo on board of the same, consisting of cotton, sugar, and dry goods in bales, and hath brought the said ship or vessel and her cargo into the port of New York, where they now are.

Secondly, That the said ship or vessel called the *Amelia* at the time of the said capture thereof, was armed with eight carriage guns, and was under the command of Citoyen Etienne Prevost, a French officer of Marine, and had on board besides the said commander thereof, eleven French mariners—that as this Libellant hath been informed, the said ship or vessal with her said cargo being the property of some person or persons to the said Libellant unknown, sailed some time since from Calcutta, an English port in the East Indies, bound for some port in Europe—That upon her said voyage she was met with and captured as a prize by a French national corvette called *La Diligente*, commanded by L. T. Dubois, who took out of her the captain and crew of the said ship *Amelia*, with all the papers relating to her and her cargo, and placed the said Ettienne Prevost and the said French mariners on board of her and ordered her to St. Domingo for adjudication, as a good and lawful prize—And that she remained in the full and peaceable possession of the French from the time of the capture thereof by them for the space of ten days, whereby this Libellant is advised that as well by the laws of nations as by the particular law of France, the said ship became and was to be considered as a French ship.

Lastly, this Proponent doth allege, propound and declare, that all and singular the premises are and were true, publick and notorious, of which due proof being made, he humbly prays the usual process and monition of this court in this behalf to be made, and that the said Etienne Prevost, and all other persons having or claiming any interest in the said ship *Amelia*, her apparel, guns, appurtenances and cargo, or any part thereof, may be cited in general and special, to answer the premises, and that right and justice may be duly administered in this behalf, and all due proceedings being had, that the same ship or vessel, her apparel, guns, appurtenances and cargo, for the causes aforesaid and others appearing, may, by the definitive sentence and decree of this honourable Court be condemned as forfeited, to be distributed as by law is provided respecting the captures made by the publick armed vessels of the United States; or if it shall appear that the same or any part or parcel thereof ought to be restored to any person or persons as the former owner or owners thereof, then that the same may be so restored upon the payment of such salvage as by law ought to be paid for the same.

RICHARD HARRISON,
Advocate for Libellant.

Answer to the foregoing Libel.

THE Claim and Answer of Hans Frederick Seaman to the Libel of Silas Talbot, Esquire, Commander of the United States ship of war the *Constitution*, on behalf as well of the United States as of himself and the officers and crew of said ship, against the ship *Amelia*, her tackle apparel, furniture and cargo, in behalf of Messrs. Chapeau Rouge and Company of Hamburg, merchants, owners of the said ship *Amelia* and her cargo.

THE said Hans Frederick Seaman, saving and reserving to himself all benefit of exception to the said Libel, answereth and saith, that the said ship *Amelia*, commanded by one Jacob Frederick Engelbrecht, as master, sailed on or about the twentieth day of February one thousand seven hundred and ninety eight from the Port of Hamburgh on a voyage to the East Indies, where she arrived safe.

That she left Calcutta commanded by the said Jacob Frederick Engelbrecht some time in the month of April last past, bound to the Port of Hamburgh aforesaid. That at the time of the said ship *Amelia* leaving Hamburgh and Calcutta as aforesaid, and at the time of her capture by the French hereinafter mentioned, she belonged with her cargo, consisting of the Articles in the said Libel mentioned, unto Messieurs Chapeau Rouge and Company, Burghers or Citizens of Hamburgh, and that the same if restored, will be the sole property of the said Chapeau Rouge and Company and of no other person. That the said ship *Amelia* was captured on or about the sixth day of September last, on the high seas as she was prosecuting her last mentioned voyage to Hamburgh aforesaid, by a French armed vessel whose name as this Claimant has understood was *la Henrietta of Rochfort*, commanded as he understood by Citizen Dubois—that the said captain Dubois, or whoever the said captain of the said armed vessel might be, took from the said ship *Amelia* the master thereof, the said Jacob Frederick Engelbrecht, and thirteen of her crew, with all her papers, leaving on board this Claimant who was mate of the said ship *Amelia*, the doctor and five other men; that the French captain sent on board of the said ship *Amelia* twelve hands, and ordered her to proceed to St. Domingo, and parted company with her the fifth day after her capture as aforesaid—that on or about the fifteenth day of September last past, the said ship *Amelia* while in possession of the French, was captured without any resistance on her part by the said ship of war the *Constitution*, and brought into the port of New York—That the *Amelia* had eight carriage guns, it being usual for all vessels engaged in the trade she was carrying on to be armed even in times of a general peace, and this Claimant further sayeth, that there being peace between France and Hamburg at the time of the capture first above mentioned, and also between the United States and Hamburg, and the United States and France, the possession of the *Amelia* by the French in the manner and for the time stated in the said Libel could neither by the laws of nations nor by the laws of France nor by those of the United States change the property of the said ship the *Amelia* and her cargo, or make the same liable to condemnation in a French court of Admiralty; that the same could not be considered as French property, therefore the said Hans Frederick Seaman, as mate, and the only officer of the said ship *Amelia* now in this port, hereby humbly claims the said ship *Amelia* and her cargo, and prays that the same may be delivered up and restored to him in the like plight and condition as at the time of the capture by the said ship the *Constitution*, for the benefit of the owners thereof, and that he may be hence dismissed with his costs and charges in this behalf sustained.

HANS FREDERICK SEAMAN.

3d November, 1799.

Libel for the restitution of a ship captured without authority.

TO THE HONOURABLE RICHARD PETERS, ESQ. &c.

The libel of Robert Findley, &c.

That your Libellants are the true owners of the SHIP WILLIAM, James Leggat master, now lying in the port of Philadelphia and within the jurisdiction of this Honourable Court.

That on the third day of May last, the said ship being on her voyage from Bremen to Potowmac river, in the state of Maryland, and within nine miles of the sea coast of the United States, received an American pilot on board for the purpose of conducting her safely up the Chesapeake bay to the place of her destination.

That after receiving the said pilot on board, she continued on the same course until she had arrived within about two miles of Cape Henry, the southern promontory of Chesapeake bay, in five fathom water, and as near the shore as the pilot thought it proper to go; when she was forcibly seized and taken into possession by a number of armed men under the command of Peter Joanene, captain of an armed schooner then coming out of Chesapeake bay, called the *Citizen Genet*, and bearing the national colours of the republick of France, as a prize to the said schooner, and hath since been detained and now is in the possession of the said Peter Joanene, who also then and there made prisoners of the captain, officers and crew of the said *ship William*, and them as prisoner doth detain.

Your Libellants not admitting that the said schooner the *Citizen Genet*, was duly commissioned and authorized to make prizes of vessels belonging to British subjects, which they pray may be inquired of, humbly insist that according to the premises, the said ship *William* was, at the time of her being so taken, upon neutral ground within the territorial jurisdiction and under the protection of the United States, who are now at peace with the King and people of Great Britain, and that the said Peter Joanene and the persons under his command had no permission or authority from or under the United States to capture British vessels within that distance from the sea coast, to which by the laws of nations and the laws of the United States, the right and jurisdiction of the United States extended.

INASMUCH, then, as the said capture and detention of the said ship *William* and the captain, officers and crew thereof are manifestly unjust and contrary to the laws of nations and the laws of the United States, your Libellants humbly pray that the said ship *William*, her cargo, tackle, apparel and furniture and all other things belonging to her may by the sentence and decree of this Honourable Court be restored to your Libellants. That the said captain, officers and crew thereof may be relieved from imprisonment for the purpose of navigating her to her destined port, and that full satisfaction may be made by the said Peter Joanene and all others concerned, as well for the said unlawful capture and detention of the said ship, as for the imprisonment of the said captain, officers and crew thereof, and all damages, charges and expenses incurred thereby.

For which end your Libellants humbly pray process of attachment, arrest and monition as in like cases is customary.

RAWLE,
Proctor pro Libellant.

June 3d, 1793.

PLEA TO JURISDICTION.

To the Honourable, &c.

The plea of Pierre Arcade Joanene, a citizen of the French Republick, in behalf of himself and all concerned in the capture of the British ship *William* and her cargo, to the Libel and petition exhibited to this Honourable Court, by &c.

The said Pierre Arcade Joanene by protestation not confessing or acknowledging any of the matters and things in the Libellant's said petition and libel contained to be true in such manner and form as the same are therein and thereby alleged, for plea to the said Libel and petition says; that he was, at the time of his attacking in an hostile manner and making prize of the said ship *William*, her cargo and people, and now is, duly commissioned by the French Republick as captain on board the armed schooner *Citizen Genet*, fitted out by and belonging to citizens of the said Republick, to attack all the enemies of the said Republick wherever he might find them, and take them prisoners with their ships, arms and property that might be found in their possession, which commission he is ready to show unto your Honour.

That he the said Pierre Arcade Joanene with his officers, seamen and mariners on board the said armed schooner *Citizen Genet*, took as prize the British ship *William* aforesaid, with the property that was found on board of her, the said ship and property belonging to some subject or subjects of the King of Great Britain, and took the people on board of her prisoners, they being subjects of the said King, and the said King and his subjects then being in open hostility and actual war with the French Republick and her citizens, and brought the said ship and property as prize and the people on board of her as prisoners into the Port of Philadelphia, and there detains on board the said schooner *Citizen Genet*.

That by the law of nations and the treaty subsisting between the United States of America and the French Republick, it doth not pertain to this Honourable Court, nor is it within the cognizance of this Court at all to interfere or hold plea respecting the said ship or property so taken as prize, or the British subjects taken on board of her as prisoners.

WHEREFORE he prays that he may be hence dismissed and the said ship and cargo discharged from arrest, &c.

Du Ponceau,
Proctor for Respondents.

11th June, 1793.

REPLICATION.

To the Honourable *Richard Peters*, Esq. &c.

The Replication of, &c. to the plea of, &c. humbly showeth :

THAT their Petition and Libel by the said Pierre Arcade Joanene in his said plea alleged ought not to be abated nor dismissed by this Honourable Court, because they say that the said ship, the *William*, her cargo, tackle, apparel and furniture, and the officers and crew thereof, were in manner aforesaid, forcibly unlawfully and unjustly seized and taken by the said Pierre Arcade Joanene, within the domain and territorial jurisdiction of the United States, then and now being at peace with the king and people of Great Britain, wherefore the said plea by the said Pierre Arcade Joanene in manner aforesaid pleaded, and the matter therein contained are not sufficient in law to abate the said petition and Libel, nor to cause the same to be dismissed.

And for default of a sufficient answer in this behalf the said Robert Findlay, &c. pray the sentence and decree of this Honourable Court according to the force, form and effect of the said petition and Libel.

RAWLE,
Proctor for Libellant.

14*th*, June 1793.

SALVAGE.

To the Honourable RICHARD PETERS *esq. judge of the District Court of the United States, in and for the District of Pennsylvania.*

The Libel of JOHN CHRISTIAN BREVOOR, master, and JOHN SCHIER SEAMAN, agent of the ship *Fair American*, now riding at anchor in the port of Philadelphia respectfully showeth:

THAT the said ship set sail from the port of Philadelphia, in the United States of America, on the 22d day of September in the year of our Lord 1798, and proceeding on her voyage from the port aforesaid to the port of the Havannah, to wit, on the eighth day of October in the year aforesaid, between the hours of nine and ten in the morning, being then to the best of their judgement, between five and six miles from the aforesaid port of the Havannah, was brought to and captured by a French privateer schooner *L'enfant de la grande Revenche*, armed and cruizing against the property of the citizens of the United States, commanded by captain Roullis. That the commander of the aforesaid privateer and his officers, after looking over the papers of the *Fair American* declared said ship and cargo good prize, and took from the ship *Fair American*, sailing as aforesaid, her officers and seamen, all except your Petitioners and Anthony Fachtman the cook, who were suffered to remain on board the said ship, and put on board from the said schooner, a prize master with six white men and two negroes, and ordered her course to be altered for Cape Francais.

That on the 16*th* day of October in the same year, between the hours of nine and ten in the morning, the said ship *Fair American* being then in latitude 28′ 45 North, and longitude 80′ 30″ West, under the command of the said French prize master, seamen and negroes, and having been under their command and controul upwards of forty eight hours, your petitioners then and there being and remaining on board the said ship *Fair American* assisted by the aforesaid Anthony Fachtman the cook, did by great labour and enterprize and at the manifest risk of their lives, re-capture and take from the hands and controul of the said French prize master, seamen, and negroes, the said ship *Fair American*, and did alter her course for the port of Charleston in the state of South Carolina, being the nearest port in the United States, where the said ship arrived in perfect safety on the 26*th* day of October, in the year aforesaid. By reason whereof the said ship and cargo were saved to the owners and all others concerned, having received nevertheless considerable damage in her rigging and sails, &c. while in possession of the French prize master and crew aforesaid.

Your petitioners further show, that the said ship *Fair American* and cargo were valued and estimated in the policies of insurance effected in Philadelphia at the time the said ship set sail from the port aforesaid, at the sum of thirty eight thousand dollars or thereabouts, and that after the said ship arrived at the port of Charleston aforesaid, she was valued and estimated with her cargo together at the sum of thirty thousand one hundred and one dollars or thereabouts :—That the cargo of the said ship alone, amounted by just valuation to the sum of twenty five-thousand and fifty-one dollars or thereabouts; that the cargo aforesaid has been sold or disposed of, so that your petitioners cannot now take benefit of process of your Honourable Court against the same.

Whereupon your petitioners pray that the process of your Honourable Court may issue to attach and seize the said ship *Fair American*, now belonging to Stephen E. Dutilh, of Philadelphia, and that by your definitive sentence the said ship may be condemned and sold, and that an adequate and reasonable proportion may be awarded to your petitioners for their labour in the premises as shall be found due to your petitioners by the laws of United States, or by the laws of nations in such cases esteemed and used—And your petitioners further pray, that process of your Honourable Court may also issue to call in Stephen E. Dutilh, owner of the said ship *Fair American* and part of the cargo aforesaid, and John Gourgon of Philadelphia, owner of the other part, and that they may be condemned to pay your Libellants such reasonable salvage as to your Honour may deem just and proper.

J. INGERSOLL,
Proctor for Libellants.

THE ANSWER OF STEPHEN DUTILH.

To the Honourable RICHARD PETERS, *Judge of the District Court, of the United States, for the District of Pennsylvania.*

THE answer of *Stephen Dutilh*, of the city of Philadelphia, merchant, to the Libel of *John Christian Brevoor* and *John Schier*, most respectfully showeth:

THAT this respondent saving to himself all and all manner of advantage to the manifest uncertainties and insufficencies in the Libellants said Libel contained, for answer thereto, or so much thereof as is material and necessary to be answered, answers and says, that well and true it is, the ship *Fair American* in said Libel mentioned, did sail from the port of Philadelphia on the 22d of September 1798, on a voyage to the Havannah, and that the said ship was valued and estimated at the sum of nine thousand dollars in the policy—and the cargo this Respondent had on board, amounted per invoice, to eleven thousand five hundred and seventy-one dollars and forty-five cents, including the premium on eleven thousand dollars insured on said goods in the Office of the Insurance Company State of Pennsylvania; that is to say, when he afterwards arrived at Charleston—And that the said ship did put into Charleston after sailing from Philadelphia as aforesaid, and that the said cargo was then and there sold and disposed of; but whether the said ship was taken by a French privateer, and whether the said ship was re-taken by the said Libellants and the said Anthony Fachtman, and in what manner and under what circumstances, this Respondent does not of his own knowledge know, and cannot set forth; and himself prays that the same may be verified by the said Libellants—And this Respondent further says, that after the said ship arrived as aforesaid at Charleston aforesaid, upon an expectation of a reward made by the said Libellants, for having re-captured the same ship in manner stated by them in the Libel aforesaid, and which this Respondent communicated to the Insurance Company of the State of Pennsylvania who had insured the said ship and the goods on board belonging to this Respondent—And the said Insurance Company requested this Respondent to pay to the said Libellants and the said Anthony Fachtman the sum of one thousand dollars, which this Respondent desired his Correspondents Messrs. Robert Hazlehurst & Co. of Charleston to do, and of which request the Respondent subjoins their letter—viz.

Insurance Office of the State of Pennsylvania.
June 3d, 1799,

" Mr. S. Dutilh,

" *Sir,*

" The Directors of the Insurance Company
" of the State of Pennsylvania having taken in-
" to consideration the spirited conduct of Cap-
" tain J. C. Brevoor and two of his men, in re-
" taking the ship *Fair American,* and conducting
" her safe into Charleston, have agreed to the
" following resolution—

" *Resolved*, That a gratuity of one thousand
" dollars be made to Captain J. C. Brevoor and
" the two other persons who assisted him in re-
" taking the ship *Fair American*, and that the
" same be paid in the following proportions :—
" To Captain Brevoor, six hundred dollars, and
" two hundred dollars to each of the other per-
" sons.—I am to request the favor of you to have
" this money paid agreeable to the above resolu-
" tion which will be allowed to you in the settle-
" ment of the insurance on the ship *Fair Ameri-
" can* and cargo. I am, for the Insurance Com-
" pany of the State of Pennsylvania,

Your obedient, humble servant,

JAMES S. COX, *President.*"

And this respondent further says, that since the arrival of the said ship at Charleston as aforesaid, the said Stephen Dutilh, then proprietor thereof, did abandon her, and also this Respondent's proportion of the cargo on board, to the Insurance Company aforesaid, and the property thereby became vested in the said Insurance Company, and the said Insurance Company did afterwards sell the same ship to the said Stephen Dutilh for the sum of five thousand and fifty dollars; and further this Respondent by desire and request of the said Insurance Company sold for their account and risque to Lewis Clapier of this city merchant, the sound flour on board said vessel, at seven dollars per barrel, and the said Lewis Clapier received in Charleston nine hundred and eighty-five barrels, for which he paid to this Respondent for account of the said

Insurance Company of the State of Pennsylvania, the sum of $6895 and further, at the request, and desire of the said Insurance Company, this Respondent, ordered the remainder of the flour and the boards to be sold by Robert Hazlehurst & Co. for account of said Insurance Company & Co. for account of the said Insurance Company, which they did and rated as per sales 156
$7051

from which sum remains to be deducted the freight on said flour and boards the sum of 3075
$3976

and since, the said ship was so purchased by him the said Stephen Dutilh, and she hath sailed on another voyage to wit, from Charleston aforesaid to Hamburgh, and she hath since returned from Hamburgh, to Philadelphia, and until her arrival at Philadelphia, no proceedings whatever have been instituted by the said Libellants, or either of them against the said ship or cargo or any part thereof, for or on account of any claim or pretended claim of Salvage.

Wherefore this Respondent humbly prays, that the Libel of the said John Christian Brevoor and John Schier, so far as it regards the said ship and this Respondent may be dismissed, and the said ship be restored to the said Stephen Dutilh, with costs, &c. &c.

RAWLE,
Proctor for STEPHEN DUTILH.

Answer of John Gourjon, &c.

To the Honourable *Richard Peters*, Esq. &c.

The answer of John Gourjon of the City of Philadelphia, respectfully showeth:

THAT this Respondent saving and reserving to himself all and all manner of advantage of exceptions to the imperfections and insufficiencies in the Libellants said Libel contained, for answer thereto, or so much thereof as is material and necessary to be answered, answers and says:

That rule it is the ship *Fair American* in the said Libel mentioned, when she sailed from Philadelphia on her voyage to the Havanna, to wit: on the 22d day of September 1798, had on board goods belonging to this Respondent amounting to twelve thousand nine hundred and seventy-three dollars; but whether the said ship was taken by a French privateer and whether she was retaken by the Libellants and by the said Anthony Fachtman, in what manner, and under what circumstances, this Respondent does not of his own knowledge know.

And this Respondent admits that the said ship did put into Charleston after sailing from Philadelphia, and he admits that part of the said goods was delivered by captain Brevoor one of the Libellants to an agent whom he himself employed to do the business of the ship, and to sell and dispose of the cargo for account of the concerned, but he denies that the whole of said goods was then and there delivered by the Libellants, or sold or disposed of as they have stated in their Libel for this Respondent—but he charges that a part of his said goods, to the amount of two thousand three hundred and nineteen dollars invoice cost, was embezzled or otherwise lost since the alledged recapture by the default of the Libellants or one of them or one of the crew of the *Fair American*, who assisted, as is alledged, in the recapture; and the residue thereof, which was sold and disposed of by the agent so employed by captain Brevoor as aforesaid, produced only a sum of six thousand four hundred and eleven dollars ninety two and an half cents, after deducting the charges.

And this Respondent further saith, that previous to instituting the present Libel, the underwriters who had ensured the said goods, directed a sum of five per cent on their respective subscriptions to be paid to the said Libellants, besides a piece of plate for captain Brevoor, amounting in the whole to nine hundred and three dollars, and fifty-five cents, for having recaptured the *Fair American* in manner stated by them int he Libel aforesaid, which compentation was accordingly offered the said captain Brevoor in behalf of himself and the Libellants, previous to exhibiting their present bill, and which the underwriters aforesaid have always been and still are ready to pay to the said Libellants.

And this respondent further saith, that on the sixteenth day of November 1798, he did abandon his portion of the cargo on board to the underwriters, and the property thereby became vested in them and was actually sold by their directions and for their account, in consequence whereof they paid him the sum of fifteen thousand and twenty two dollars and sixty five cents, being the full amount of their subscriptions after deducting the charges, &c.

And this Respondent further saith that the said goods, so far as the same were or might have been delivered to the agent so employed at Charleston were then sold and disposed of with the assent of captain Brevoor, and that no proceedings whatever were then instituted by the said Libellants, or either of them against the same, for on account of any claim of salvage.

And as to the residue of the said Libel praying process to attach the person of this Respondent in order that he may be compelled to pay the salvage claimed by the said Libellants, this Respondent saith that this Honourable Court ought not to have cognizance of the said plea as affecting the person of this Respondent, because this Honourable Court hath not jurisdiction thereof, and this he is prepared to verify.— And therefore he prays that this Honourable Court will not further proceed with respect to the residue of the said Libel, praying process to attach the body of this Respondent—prays that the bill of the Libellants so far as it regard him may be dismissed with costs, &c.

J. GOURJON.

MOYLAN, *Proctor for Respondent.*
18*th* July, 1800.

Protest to Evidence

The respondent, Stephen Dutilh, objects to the commission issued out of this Honourable Court directed to *Wm. H. D. &c.* and the depositions of *F. C. M.* taken by the said Commissioners and returned to this Court, being read in evidence so far as affects the right and interest of the said Stephen Dutilh, and issue joined between the said *J. B.* and *J. S.* and the said *S. D.* and doth protest against the same being read in evidence so far as it may in any way affect him in the defence he hath made, and the right and interest he hath in the matter in controversy.

M. RAWLE,
for S. DUTILH, *Respondent.*

The above objection having been offered to the Court, and a motion having been made for leave to enter the same on the minutes of the Court, and his Honour the Judge having refused permission to enter the same, the advocates for the said Stephen Dutilh, Respondent, do protest against the conduct of the said Judge in this particular.

LEWIS } *Advocates for*
RAWLE } S. DUTILH *Respondent.*

29*th* July, 1800.

The Replication

To the Honourable RICHARD PETERS, *Esq. &c.*

The Replication of John Brevoor, master, and John Schier, seaman, Libellants, against the ship *Fair American*, to the separate answer of Stephen H. Dutilh and John Gourjon, Respondents, humbly showeth :

THAT your Libellants, saving and reserving to themselves all and all manner of advantage and exceptions, to the manifest imperfections and insufficiencies in the said Respondents' separate answers contained, for answer thereto, or so much thereof as it is material and necessary for them to make answer, they answer and say : That inasmuch as your Libellants are called upon to certify, that the ship *Fair American* was captured and taken by a French Privateer, and re-captured by the Libellants with the assistance of Anthony Fachtman, the cook, and in manner and form, and it is more fully set forth, and made known in the Libel of your said Libellants ; they aver that the proofs on which they rely to confirm and verify the said capture and re-capture are here in Court ready to be produced. And you Libellants further answering, say, that well and true it is, as set forth in the separate answer of the Respondent, Stephen Dutilh, that the said Respondent did desire his correspondents, Messrs. R. Hazlehurst & Co. of Charleston to pay, &c. which said sum your Libellants acknowledge to have received, &c. but your Libellants affirm that the said sum was not paid them, until the moment when they were about entering on a voyage, which prevented them from taking any legal steps at that time, to testify their dissatisfaction at the smallness and insufficiency of the compensation made; and further your Libellants affirm, that they have always been dissatisfied with the aforesaid sum, considered as a reward for their labour, risk and trouble, in retaking the ship *Fair American* from the hands of the enemy and restoring her with her cargo to the concerned.

And your Libellants further answering (*replying*) say, that well and true it is, as set forth, &c. that the underwriters, &c. did direct a sum of five per-cent, &c. but which they refused and still do refuse to accept; deeming the same a compensation altogether inadequate and insufficient to indemnify your Libellants for their labour, risk and trouble as aforesaid.

And your Libellants further answering (*replying*) say, that well and true it is, that no proceedings, &c. but your Libellants deny that they have ever renounced or abandoned their just title to salvage, by reason of any such delay, and this they are prepared to verify.

And your Libellants further answering (*replying*) say, that for as much as in the separate answer of the Respondents, John Gourjon, they are charged with having embezzled, &c. your Libellants deny that they have, &c.

WHEREFORE your Libellants, asserting and maintaining that the several facts and things alleged and set forth in their aforesaid Libel are true and sufficient to ground their title to the salvage and indemnity therein sought—humbly pray that their claim in this respect may be sustained, and that they may be allowed such reasonable salvage as to your Honour may seem just and proper.

          INGERSOLL, } *Proctors for*
          ADAMS,   } *Libellants.*
22*d* July, 1800.

BOTTOMRY.

TO THE HONOURABLE, &c.

The Libel of George Barclay, of the city of London, merchant, John Drury of the same place, Banker, and John Mangles of Wapping in the county of Middlesex, and Kingdom of Great Britain, merchant; against the ship *Lavinia*, her freight, tackle and apparel, against William Vicary, now or late master of the said ship, and against Peter Blight now or late owner thereof, and George Blight, Thomas Murgatroyd and William Cole, assignees of the said Peter Blight, respectfully showeth:

THAT your Libellants did on the 21*st* day of May A. D. 1800, lend on Bottomry on the ship *Lavinia*, her freight, tackle and apparel to the said William Vicary the sum of one thousand four hundred and twenty pounds two shillings and six pence sterling money of Great Britain, the said ship *Lavinia* whereof the said William Vicary was then master, then lying and being at the port of London, being a foreign port, and none of the owners of the same ship being at or near the said port, the said captain being otherwise unable to procure the necesssary monies to refit and victual his said ship, and compleat his intended voyage, for which sum of one thousand four hundred and twenty pounds two shillings and six-pence, the said William Vicary did on the said 21st day of May 1800, by a due and lawful Instrument of Bottomry and Hypothecation bearing date the same day and year, a copy whereof is hereto annexed to which your Libellants pray leave to refer as part of this Libel, Hypothecate the said ship the *Lavinia*, with her freight, tackle, and apparel to your Libellants for the payment of the sum of one thousand seven hundred and sixteen pounds and five shillings sterling money, being the same sum with interest, within seventeen days after the arrival of the same ship at the port of Philadelphia—And your Libellants do aver that the said ship the *Lavinia* did arrive at the said port of Philadelphia, the 18th day of July last past, where she still lies, and the said term of seventeen days hath fully expired, yet the said sum of one thousand seven hundred and sixteen pounds five shillings remains wholly unpaid.

Wherefore your Libellants pray the process of this Honourable Court, to attach the said ship the *Lavinia*, her freight, tackle and apparel and to cite and admonish, the said William Vicary, Peter Blight, George Blight, Thomas Murgatroyd and William Cole, and all others concerned to show cause, if any they have, why the said vessel with her tackle and apparel should not be sold and the said freight paid to your Libellants to satisfy their demand aforesaid.

W. RAWLE,
Proctor for the Libellants.

HYPOTHECATION.

To the Honourable, &c.

THE joint and several answers of Wm. Vicary, late master of the ship *Lavinia*, Peter Blight, the late owner thereof, and George Blight, Thomas Murgatroyd and Wm. Cole assignees of the said Peter Blight Respondents to the Libel of Geo. Barclay of the city of London, Merchant, John Drury of the same place, Banker, and John Mangles of Wapping in the County of Middlesex, and Kingdom of Great Britain, Merchant, Libellants.

The said respondents now, and at all times hereafter, saving and reserving to themselves, all and all manner of benefit and advantage of exception to the manifold incertainties and imperfections in the said Libel of the Libellants contained, for answer thereunto or unto so much thereof as materially concerns them, to make answer unto, answer and say—that the said ship *Lavinia*, in the said Libel mentioned, was assigned and transferred by the said Peter Blight to Z. R. Read, (in whose name she is duly registered) on the 20*th* of

December 1799, and freight and allowances aforesaid, when received from the Libellants, and not with a view to pledge or Hypothecate the said ship for the payment thereof, the Libellants well knowing the premises, but regardless of their agreement made and entered into as aforesaid, refused to pay to the said William Vicary the amount of the said freight and allowances, or any part thereof, by reason of which refusal, the said William Vicary became unable to pay or satisfy the several persons from whom he had obtained credit as aforesaid, for the use of said ship, and was apprehensive that such creditors would institute suits against him personally, as well as attachments against the said ship *Lavinia*, in order to recover the sums respectively due them. And the said Respondents further answering, say, that the said Libellants taking advantage of the embarrassment, which the said William Vicary was thus involved, in consequence of their refusal to to perform the agreement by them entered into as aforesaid, and designing to compel the said Peter Blight or his assignees *to pay to the said Libellants* a further sum over and above the proceeds of the said cargo, under colour of an Hypothecation of the said ship *Lavinia*, offered to supply the said William Vicary with a sum of money equal in amount to the debts contracted as aforesaid for the *expenses, repairs* and *victualling* of the said ship *Lavinia,* provided he would execute the Instruments of Bottomry and Hypothecation, bearing date the *21st* May 1800, in the said Libel of the Libellants mentioned. That the said William Vicary being destitute of all pecuniary means in consequence of the violation as aforesaid, on the part of the Libellants of their said agreements was compelled to accept the said offer, but previously to the acceptance thereof (to wit, on the 17*th* of May 1800,) he made and entered his Protest in due form, before a Notary Public, a copy whereof is hereunto annexed marked *C*, and to which the said Respondents crave leave to refer as a part of this their answer—And the said Respondents further answering say, that true it is, that the said William Vicary did, under the circumstances before stated, receive from the Libellants the sum of one thousand four hundred pounds, thirteen shillings and two pence sterling money, equal in amount to the debts and disbursements specified in the copies of the accounts *D* and *E* hereunto annexed, to which the said Respondents crave leave to refer as a part of this their answer; and also thereupon executed the said Instrument of Bottomry and Hypothecation, bearing date the 21*st* of May 1800, for one thousand seven hundred and sixteen pounds five shillings sterling, whereof a copy is annexed to the said Libel of the Libellants. But these Respondents aver, that the said Instrument of Bottomry and Hypothecation was executed after the Libellants had refused to perform the said agreement, and merely on account of the embarrassment and necessity arising from such refusal, and under the apprehension which the said William Vicary felt of being arrested unless he complied with the requisition of the said Libellants.—And the said Respondents further answering, say, that beside protesting as aforesaid, on the said 17*th* May 1800, against the necessity for granting such Bottomry and Hypothecation, which necessity was produced as aforesaid by the refusal of the said Libellants to perform their said agreement, the said William Vicary, caused it expressly to be recited in the said Instrument of Bottomry and Hypothecation as an inducement to the granting thereof, that he had delivered all the said cargo of the *Lavinia*, to the Libellants, as assignees of the said Henry H. Fentham, without being able to recover any part of the proceeds of the said cargo, or any freight for the same; and further obtained from S. W. Waderson, the agent and Attorney of the said Libellants, on their behalf, a declaration and agreement in writing, that in case the sum of sixteen pounds, ten shillings sterling, be paid to the said Libellants in London, at any time within the space of six months, from the date of such last mentioned declaration and agreement, they will accept the same in lieu and full satisfaction, of the whole of the said supposed Bottomry debt as will fully appear by the said last mentioned declaration and agreement, bearing date the 21*st* of May 1800—a copy whereof marked *F* is hereunto annexed and to which the said Respondents crave leave to refer as a part of this their answer. And the Respondents further answering, say and aver, that the money so paid by the Libellants to the said William Vicary, and on the receipt whereof, under the necessity and apprehension aforesaid, the said instrument of Bottomry and Hypothecation was executed as aforesaid, was not the proper money of the said Libellants, but that the same was part of the proceeds of the said cargo of the said ship *Lavinia*, which came to the said Libellants, as assignees of the said H. H. Fentham after the delivery of the said cargo to them by the said William Vicary, upon the agreement and condition aforesaid, and which money the said Libellants were bound to pay to the said William Vicary out of the proceeds of the said cargo for the uses of the said ship *Lavinia* as aforesaid without any Bottomry, Hypothecation or security whatsoever. And the said Respondents further aver, that the said Libellants did not, with the proceeds, or any part of the proceeds of the said cargo, pay to the owner of the said ship *Lavinia*, or to the said William Vicary, or to any other person for the said owner, the freight, commission, expences, offtaking and keeping possession and delivery of the said cargo, duties and all other charges and expenses relating to the said cargo, otherwise than is above set forth before they applied such proceeds in or towards satisfaction of bills or other debts and engagements accepted, contracted or made by the said H. H. Fentham, on account of the said Peter Blight, if ever they have so applied the said proceeds, which the said Respondents do not omit—And the said Respondents further answering say, that true it is, that the said ship *Lavinia* arrived at the port of Philadelphia, on the 18*th* of July, last past, and still lies in the said port, but they deny that the said ship and the freight thereof are liable for the payment of the said sum of one thousand seven hundred and sixteen pounds, five shillings, in the said Libel mentioned or any part thereof; and they insist that even if the said ship and freight were so liable, that the same is not due and payable until the expiration of six months from the 21st of May 1800, being the date of the said declaration and agreement, signed as aforesaid by the said S. W. Wadeson on behalf of the said Libellants.——— And the said Respondents pray that the said Libel may be dismissed with costs, &c.

A. J. DALLAS,
Proctor for Respondents.

REPLICATION.

To the Honourable, &c.

THE replication of George Barclay, John Drury and John Mangles, to the joint and several answers of William Vicary, Peter Blight, George Blight, Thomas Murgatroyd and William Cole, or to so much thereof as it is material or necessary for them to reply unto the said Replicants saving and reserving all benefit and advantage of exception to the uncertainties and insufficiencies in the said answer contained, and all benefit of the matters of facts therein *stated,* acknowledged and confessed for Replication to so much of the said answer as these Repliants deny to be true, propound and say, that the said ship *Lavinia,* at the time of the said Bottomry and Hypothecation in their Libel set forth and at the time of the arrival of the said ship at the Port of

Philadelphia aforesaid, was the property of the said Peter Blight, and that the assignment of the said ship, by the said Peter Blight to Z. R. Read in the said answer mentioned, if any such was made, which the Repliants do not admit, was not bona fide, but in trust for the said Peter Blight, to secure the same from legal process and faudulent and void as against the creditors of the said Peter Blight, and that the register of the said ship in the name of the said Z. R. Read, if the name was so registered, which these Repliants do not admit, was done in collusion with the said Peter Blight for similar fraudulent purposes, and the assignment of the residue of the said Peter Blight's interest in the said ship, to the said *G. B. T. M.* and *W. C.* if any such there were, which these Repliants do not admit, was not bona fide, but fraudulent, collusive and void, against the creditors of the said Peter Blight, *and all which these Repliants are ready to prove*, without that, that the said ship *Lavinia*, at any time was or now is the just and lawful property of the said Z. R. Read in the Repliant's said answer mentioned.

And these Respondents further say, that true it is, the said ship belonging as these Repliants contend, to the said Peter Blight, sailed from the Port of Philadelphia, in the District of Pennsylvania bound to the Port of London, and consigned to Henry Hale Fentham, with a cargo on board belonging also to the said Peter Blight, and that the said ship put into the Port of Plymouth, and the said William Vicary went by land to London, and that before the arrival of the said William Vicary at London, the said Henry H. Fentham was declared a Bankrupt, and the said George Barclay, John Drury, and John Mangles, were appointed his assignees, and as such requested the delivery of the said cargo to them as representing the said bankrupt, the consignee thereof. And these Repliants confessing, the said agreement in the said answer mentioned and refused to, dated the 10*th* day of February 1800, say that they have in all things performed and fulfilled the said agreement, according to the true intent and meaning thereof, wherein it ought to be or could be performed, the subject matter of the said cargo and the object to which the covenants in the said contracts entered into by the Repliants premarily allude, being the cargo *then* on board said ship at Plymouth, the Repliants engaging to apply the nett proceeds of the said cargo, after paying freight of the said cargo, the commissions on the sales of the said cargo, expences of taking and keeping possession and delivering the said cargo, brought from Philadelphia, as hereinafter mentioned without that, that these Repliants in any respect infringed or broke the same, inasmuch as these Repliants were not thereby obliged to pay or advance or become responsible for any part of the said ship's expenses, others than as above enumerated, and except so far as the same related to the said outward cargo of the said ship, and the whole of the nett proceeds of the said cargo were to be applied according to the said agreement after discharging the duties and all other charges and expenses, relating to the said cargo in or towards satisfaction of bills, or other engagements accepted, contracted, or made by the said Henry H. Fentham, on account of Peter Blight of Philadelphia——And these Repliants did so apply the *entire* proceeds of the said cargo and thereby did in fact, so far as the same extended, pay the debts of the said Peter Blight, then proprietor of the said ship and cargo, and being so proprietor of both, there was no freight due or payable on the same goods and cargo except for lighterage which these Replicants have fully discharged, although if the said ship had been unable to come round from Plymouth to London, it would have been necessary to have freighted another vessel, for the payment of which the Repliants by the said agreements would have been liable—And these Repliants deny that the said William Vicary, with the privity and concurrence of these Repliants or any agent of theirs, having authority to that purpose, did procure credits for the said ship, with a view, or with an expectation, encouraged by them, to be reimbursed out of monies to be received from the Repliants under the said agreements, nor did these Repliants ever refuse to pay any freight due, or which they at any time, had represented as due or to become due, as the freight of said cargo, or practice any deceit with the said William Vicary, or other person upon the same subject; and the said Repliants aver that upon the representation of the said William Vicary, that the sum in the said Bottomry contained, was necessary to pay and

Y

discharge the expences repairs and victualling of the said ship, other than that what respected the said outward cargo and that without such repairs and other expences as aforesaid last mentioned, the ship could not have performed, and compleated her voyage from London to Philadelphia, nor had the said William Vicary, either money or goods belonging to the owner of the said ship by which he could have paid the said necessary expences, nor was he able to raise the same by bills or otherwise on the credit of the owner; and that these Repliants by their advances enabled the said ship to complete her return voyage, and that such advances were made by them for their purpose, upon the express stipulation of the said William Vicary, the master of the said ship, that he would pledge and Hypothecate the said ship for the security and reimbursement thereof in case of safe arrival, and that the money in the said Bottomry and Hypothecation mentioned, was the proper money of these Repliants and not the proceeds of the said cargo, the same having been applied agreeable to the contract that was entered into as aforesaid, between these Repliants and the said William Vicary as aforesaid.

And these Repliants confessing the said agreement in the Respondents said answer mentioned and referred to, dated 20*th* May 1800, deny that it does in any way or manner affect their right to sue and prosecute for the recovery of the amount due upon and contained in the said Bottomry and Hypothecation.

WHEREFORE these Repliants pray as in their Libel they before have prayed, that by the sentence and decree of this Honourable Court the said Brigantine, her tackle, furniture and apparel may be condemned and sold to satisfy the Libellants' demand, with the costs, and charges and so, forth.

REJOINDER.

The Rejoinder of William Vicary, Peter Blight, George Blight, Thomas Murgatroyd, and William Cole, the Respondents to the Replication of George Barclay, John Drury, and John Mangle, the Libellants in his cause.

The said Rejoinants saving and reserving all benefit and advantage of exception to the uncertainties and insufficencies in the said Replication contained, and all benefit of the matters of fact therein acknowledged and confessed, for rejoinder to so much of the replication, as these rejoinants deny to be true, they propound, and say: That the ship *Lavinia* in the said Replication and proceedings mentioned, was not at the time of the Bottomry in the said Libel mentioned nor at the time of her arrival at Philadelphia aforesaid, the property of the said Peter Blight, but that the same was at that time the property of the said Z. R. Read, and had been previously assigned and transferred to, and registered in the name of the said Z. R. Read, to wit, on the 22d day December 1799, *bond fide* for a valuable consideration and not fraudulently with a view to secure the same from legal process, nor in collusion between the said Peter Blight, and Z. R. Read as appears by the assignment and registry, copies whereof are hereunto annexed—And these Rejoinants further propound, and say, that all the property, interest, claim and demand of the said Peter Blight, (if any he had) of, in and to, the said ship *Lavinia*, were further transferred and vested in the said George Blight, Thomas Murgatroyd and William Cole, or some or one of them by the Deeds of Assignment in the answer of these Rejoinants mentioned, some or one of them, for the uses and on the condition in the said deeds of agreement, some or one. of them specified, before the Bottomry in the said Libel mentioned, and the arrival of the said ship *Lavinia* at the port of Philadelphia, as aforesaid— And the said deeds of agreement were made *bonâ fidé* without fraud or collusion for the benefit of the creditors of the said Peter Blight therein specified. And these Rejoinants further propound and say, that before the date of the said Bottomry and they believe at the time of entering into the said agreement on the tenth day of February 1800, the said Libellants were fully acquainted with the ownership of the said *Lavinia*, and that they have not fulfilled the said agreements according to the true intent and meaning thereof, wherein it ought and could be performed in as much as they did not, and have not paid the freight, commissions and expences in the said agreement mentioned, although such payment ought to have been made, and the said agreement could in that respect have been performed and fulfilled. And these Rejoinants further propound and say, that the said Libellants were by the said agreement of the 10th February 1800, obliged to pay the freight, commission and expences therein mentioned, out of the proceeds of the said cargo, and before the same could be applied towards satisfaction of the bills or other debts and engagements accepted and contracted, or made by the said Henry H. Fentham, on account of the said Peter Blight; and that the said ship *Lavinia*, and her cargo would not have been delivered to the said Libellants, but in consideration of their promise, and agreement to pay the said freight, commission and expences as aforesaid, and with a view to apply the monies received on such payment to the equipment and expences of the said ship *Lavinia*, for her return voyage to Philadelphia aforesaid. And these Rejoinants further propound and say, that the freight for the said cargo, was due and payable unto the said Z. R. Read, George Blight, Thomas Murgatroyd and William Cole, or some or one of them as owners, or owner of the said ship *Lavinia*, by virtue of the transfer and assignment aforesaid, and the Rejoinants further propound and say, that the Libellants, did refuse to pay the freight due for the said outward cargo, of the said ship *Lavinia*, and that the said William Vicary, was compelled in the manner and for the reasons set forth in the answer, of these Respondents to accept the money, in the said pretended Bottomry, or Hypothecation mentioned, and to execute the said Instrument as aforesaid. But these Rejoinants say, that before and at the time and subsequent to the execution of the said Instrument, the Libellants were possessed of goods, wares, merchandise and money, belonging to the said Peter Blight, owner of the said outward cargo, whereby and wherewith all the expences for the return voyage for the said ship, might and ought to have been defrayed and paid, if as the said Libellants pretend (but which these Rejoinants do not admit) the said ship had been then the property of the said Peter Blight, without compelling the said William Vicary, to execute any Bottomry or Hypothecation therefor. And these Rejoinants further propound and say, that the money advanced by the Libellants, as aforesaid was not advanced upon the express stipulation of the said William Vicary, that he would pledge and Hypothecate the said ship, nor upon the condition, securing and reimbursing the same in case of the safe arrival of the said ship *Lavinia* at the port of Philadelphia, but it was advanced under the circumstances by these Rejoinants in their answer and in their Rejoinder set forth, upon a stipulation also that the said William Vicary should bind himself, his executors and administrators to reimburse the same. And these Rejoinants further propound and say, that the money in the said pretended Bottomry and Hypothecation mentioned, was advanced at a time when the said outward cargo or the proceeds thereof remained in the hands of the Libellants, and before the same, or any part thereof, was or could be applied agreeably to the said contract of the 10*th* of February 1800, and that the money so advanced to the said William

Vicary was payable, and ought to have been paid out of the proceeds of the outward cargo before any other application thereof; and that the said Libellants, having the said cargo, or the proceeds thereof in their hands, were bound by the said contract of the 10*th* of February 1800, to make up such prior payment, without any Bottomry or Hypothecation to secure a reimbursement thereof, and that the money so advanced to the said William Vicary, was part of the proceeds of the said outward cargo, but if at the time of advancing the same, it was the proper money of the Libellants, these Rejoinants propound and say, the same has been or ought to have been since retained or reimbursed by the said Libellants out of the proceeds of the said cargo. And these Rejoinants further propound and say, that the agreement of the 21*st* of May 1800, acknowledged in the said Replication of the said Libellants, would affect the right of the said Libellants to sue and prosecute for the recovery of the amount due upon the said Bottomry or Hypothecation, if any thing was thereupon due (which these Rejoinants do not admit) for the term of six months, from the date of the said agreement of the 2*d* of May, 1800 : and that by reason of the Libellants suing upon the said Bottomry or Hypothecation before the expiration of the said term of six months, these Rejoinants would be deprived (according to their respective rights) of the benefit and advantage of making the payment of one thousand six hundred and ten pounds, in the said last mentioned agreement, stipulated in full satisfaction of the

FORFEITURE

Of a ship on account of her being falsely registered.

UNITED STATES OF AMERICA, MARYLAND DISTRICT, SS.

To the Honourable JAMES WINCHESTER, *Judge of the District Court, of the United States, for the Maryland District.*

IN the name and on the behalf of the United States of America, Zebulon Hollingsworth, Attorney of the United States for Maryland District, cometh into Court here in his proper person, and giveth the Court here to understand and be informed, that heretofore, to wit, on the 25th November 1801, at the Port of Baltimore, in Maryland District, a certain Aquilla Brown, a citizen of the United States of America and of the City of Baltimore, being a part owner of a certain ship called the *Anthony Mangin,* appeared before Robert Purviance, Collector of the Customs for the United States of America at the Port of Baltimore in Maryland District, he the said Robert Purviance being then and there the officer authorised by law to make registry of the said ship; and the said Aquilla Brown then and there, to wit, on the day and year aforesaid, at the District aforesaid, made oath before the said Robert Purviance on the Holy Evangels of Almighty God, that he the said Aquilla Brown was the sole owner of the said ship called the *Anthony Mangin*, the said oath being then and there made by the said Aquilla Brown, and so as aforesaid administered by the said Robert Purviance, Collector as aforesaid, in order to the registry of the said ship, and with the intent to obtain, and for the purpose of obtaining a register for the said ship, pursuant to the statue of the United States in such case made and provided. And the said Attorney in the name and on behalf of the said United States doth aver, and in fact say, that the said fact in the said oath alleged, that the said Aquilla Brown, was the sole owner of the said ship called the *Anthony Mangin*, within the knowledge of the said Aquilla Brown so swearing as aforesaid was not true, to wit, on the day and year aforesaid, at the District aforesaid, but the said Attorney in the name and on the behalf of the said United States doth in fact aver and say, that the said fact so alleged in the said oath was false and untrue, and that within the knowledge of the said Aquilla Brown, a certain Herman Henry Hackeman, an alien, and not a citizen of the United States of America, was part owner of the said ship called the *Anthony Mangin*, at the time of making the said oath by the said Aquilla Brown as aforesaid, with the intent and for the purpose aforesaid, and in order to the re-

gistry of the said ship, to wit, on the day and year aforesaid, at the district aforesaid, for which causes the said Robert Purviance, Collector as aforesaid, hath seized the said ship, her tackle, apparel and furniture, as by law forfeited.——
Wherefore the said Attorney prayeth the advice of the Court here in the premises, and that due process of law may issue against the said ship, her tackle, apparel and furniture, and that due proclamation with monition may issue in this behalf to cite and admonish all persons to be and appear at a day and place by your honour to be named to show cause, if any they have, why the said ship called the *Anthony Mangin*, her tackle, apparel and furniture should not be condemned and sold, and the money arising from said sale to be distributed according to law, and that she be so condemned and sold and the money so distributed, *prayeth*.

ZEB. HOLLINGSWORTH,
Attorney for the U. S. for Maryland Dist.

CLAIM AND ANSWER.

And now comes here Thomas W. Norman by Luther Martin, his Proctor, and claims the said ship, her tackle apparel and furniture, and for his claim and answer unto the said Libel, he saith that the said ship was originally built in the State of Virginia, and that when she was completely fitted for sea she was registered as the sole property of the said Brown, and that the sea letter obtained for the said ship on her first voyage was obtained for her as the sole property of the said Brown. This Claimant further saith, that on the voyage which the said ship first made, was to England and back to Baltimore, and which was the only voyage performed by her while she was owned by said Brown, this Claimant was master of said ship, and that a considerable part of her cargo was on freight, and that the whole of the said freight was, in England, applied to the use of the said Brown alone, and that on the return of the said ship to the Port of Baltimore, this Claimant still continuing master thereof, the freight which became due on the return voyage was received by the assignees of the said Brown, he having in the intermediate time been declared a bankrupt, and by them applied to the use of the creditors of the said Brown. This Claimant further answering saith, that upon the return of the said ship to the said Port of Baltimore, she was taken into the possession of the said assignees as having been the property of the said Brown, and was there publickly advertised in the newspapers of that city for sale as the property of the said Brown, and was so sold as such in the city of Baltimore at publick auction, and, as this Claimant believes with the privity and knowledge of the said Robert Purviance, and the other officers of the customs for the Port of Baltimore, and that at the said sale, the said ship &c. was purchased by one Michael Saunderson, a citizen of the United States, he being the highest bidder, to whom a register was duly granted by the said Robert Purviance, collector as aforesaid at the Port of Baltimore. This Claimant further answering saith, that while the said Michael Saunderson was owner of the said ship, she made a voyage to England and returned again to the Port of Baltimore, and that upon the return of the said ship to the Port of Baltimore this Claimant purchased the said ship from the said Michael Saunderson, and duly obtained a register for the said ship from the said Robert Purviance Collector, as aforesaid at the Port of Baltimore aforesaid, and that the said Robert Purviance, and the other officers of the customs at the said Port when the register was granted to the said Michael Saunderson, and also when the register was granted to this Claimant well knew that the said ship was the same for which the said Brown had obtained a register as aforesaid. This Claimant further answering saith, that after he had thus obtained a register for the said ship, be prosecuted one voyage with her to England, and from thence to the Port of Baltimore; immediately after her arrival at which port she was seized as aforesaid, and that he doth not know, believe or admit, that the said ship was part owned by the said Hackman or any other person except the said Brown at the time when the said Brown made oath as aforesaid. Wherefore the said Norman doth claim the said ship, her tackle, &c. as his property and prays that the same may be restored to him, and that he may have his costs in this matter sustained and his damages occasioned by the seizure and detention of the said ship, &c. so unlawfully made, to him decreed, &c.

LUTHER MARTIN,
for the Claimant.

14th May, 1803, A warrant of appraisement being issued agreeably to the provisions of the act of Congress, and the ship valued by three persons appointed by the court, the Claiment filed a bond, with condition that he should " pay the valuation, in case the ship should be condemned and in all things comply with the final judgment to be rendered in the premises."

To the Honourable RICHARD PETERS, *Esq. &c.*

THE Libel of Phineas Bond, Consul General of his Majesty the king of the United Kingdom of Great Britain and Ireland in the United States of America for the Middle and Southern States of the same, respectfully showeth:

That some time about the —— day of —— last, as this Libellant hath been informed and believes, a certain brigantine, the name whereof is unknown to him, laden with a cargo of Sugar, Rum and Coffee, put up in bags, and in hogsheads, tierces and barrels, marked *T.* and *C.* the property of certain subjects of the king of the said United Kingdom, sailed from the Island of Barbadoes bound to the port of Charleston, in the State of South Carolina, consigned to Messrs. Tunno and Cox, Merchants of Charleston aforesaid. That, while lawfully and peaceably pursuing the said voyage, the said brigantine was, on or about the —— day of —— last, violently and forcibly taken on the high seas by a certain privateer, manned by persons calling themselves citizens of the French Republic, and by them carried, together with the cargo aforesaid, to St Jago de Cuba, being within the Dominions of his Majesty the king of Spain, between whom and the king of the said United Kingdom, there then was and still is peace and amity.—— That the said cargo was unladen from the said brigantine at St. Jago de Cuba aforesaid, and there reshipped on board a certain other brigantine called the *Potowmac*, commanded by captain —— Tupper, bound to the port of Baltimore in the State of Maryland. That the said cargo, after the arrival of the said brigantine *Potowmac* at Baltimore aforesaid, was there again unladen and reshipped on board the schooner *Minerva*, captain Wilson, bound to the port of Philadelphia. That seventeen hogsheads of Rum, two hundred and eight bags of Coffee and fifty-two hogsheads and tierces, and seventy barrels of Sugar, or the greater part thereof, part of the said cargo, have been brought into the port of Philadelphia, in the District of Pennsylvania, and within the jurisdiction of this honourable Court, and are now there in the possession of a certain John Gardiner, junior, of the said city of Philadelphia, Merchant. That the Libellant hath been informed and believes that no sentence or decree of condemnation hath ever been pronounced against the said cargo or any part of it or against the brigantine in which it was shipped from Barbadoes bound to Charleston aforesaid, by any Court of lawful jurisdiction, and the Rum, Sugar and Coffee aforesaid, were brought as aforesaid into the United States and into the port of Philadelphia, in order that the same might be sold, in manifest violation of amity and friendship so happily subsisting between the said United States, and the king of the said United Kingdom, and of the neutrality of the said United States.

The said Libellant, therefore prays, the aid of the process of this Honourable Court, to arrest and attach the said Rum, Coffee and Sugar, and that the same may be decreed to be restord to him, on behalf of the owners thereof, subjects of the king of United Kingdom aforesaid, togetherwith damages to be paid by the said John Gardiner, jr. for the unjust detention of the same.

W. TILGHMAN,
Proctor for the Libellant.

CLAIM.

THE said John Gardiner, junior, a citizen of the United States of America, and Consignee of said Goods, on behalf of —— Taggart and Thomas Caldwell, of the city of Baltimore, in the State of Maryland, Merchants and citizens of the United States, claims the said Goods and Merchandizes, as the sole and absolute property, Goods and Chattels of the said —— Taggart, and Caldwell, at the time of the arrest and seizure thereof by the Libellant, and claims, also, on their behalf, all such costs, charges, damages and expenses as have arisen, or shall, or may arise by reason of the seizure and detention of the same.

JOHN GARDINER, JUNIOR.

RECUSANT OWNERS.

To the Honourable RICHARD PETERS *esq. judge of the District Court of the United States, in and for the District of Pennsylvania.*

THE Petition of Willings and Francis, and Samuel S. Cooper, respectfully showeth:

That your Petitioners are owners of three fourths parts of the brigantine *Amelia.* That your Petitioners are desirous of sending the same vessel on a voyage to Saint Sebastians, in the Kingdom of Spain, *and from* Saint Sebastians back to Philadelphia.*

That the remaining one fourth part of the same vessel belongs to Peter Blight, of the city of Philadelphia, Merchant, who refuses to join in the said voyage, or to suffer the same vessel to sail on your Petitioners account.

Your Petitioners therefore respectfully pray that this Honourable Court, conforming to the established Law and usage, of the Admiralty,

---

* The words in Italicks were inserted in the Libel after answer filed, by consent.

will grant a citation, returnable at the next Court day to the said Peter Blight, to show cause if any he has, why your Petitioners should not be admitted to give security for the safe return of the same vessel, and thereupon proceed with her on the said intended voyage.

WILLINGS & FRANCIS,
SAMUEL S. COOPER.

16th August, 1800.

REPLICATION.

To the Honourable, &c.

THE answer of Peter Blight, of the City of Philadelphia, Merchant, to the Petition of Willings and Francis, and Samuel S. Cooper, respectfully showeth:

That the Respondent admits that the said Petitioners are owners of three fourth parts of the brigantine *Amelia*, but this Respondent avers that before the filing of the said petition, he had assigned all his property, real and personal whatsoever and wheresoever, to George Blight, Thomas Murgatroyd and William Cole, in trust for the benefit of his creditors, and therefore he is no longer owner of the remaining one fourth part of the same vessel, nor entitled, without the discretions, authorities and approbation of his said trustees to join in the voyage, in the said petition mentioned, or to suffer the said vessel to sail on the said Petitioners ownaccount.

And this Respondent further answering saith, that he believes his said trustees would be willing (as he himself would be,) to join in sending the said vessel, on any voyage for the general benefit of the owners, provided such voyage was truly and fully made known to them; but the said Petitioners have not set forth to what place or places it is intended to send the said vessel after her arrival at Saint Sebastians; and this Respondent has been informed and avers, that it is not intended that the said vessel should return from Saint Sebastians immediately to Philadephia, but that she should be employed by the said Petitioners, in a long, hazardous and circuitous voyage, not mentioned or described in the said petition.

And this Respondent further answering saith, that the Petitioners have not in their said petition offered to purchase, the late share of the Respondent in the said vessel assigned as aforesaid, to his said trustees, nor have they offered to sell the said vessel, and distribute the money among the owners in proportion, nor have they offered to give security for paying any part of the profits of the voyage or freight of the said vessel, to this Respondent, or his said trustees, nor have they offered to give security for the return of the said vessel within a limited time.

Wherefore and because this Court has not jurisdiction of the case, the same not being a civil cause of Admiralty and Maritime jurisdiction, inasmuch as the said vessel was at the time of filing the said petition, and now is within the body or District of Pennsylvania, and not upon the High Seas. The Respondent prays that the said petition may be dismissed with costs, &c.

A. J. DALLAS,
Proctor for the Respondent.

DECREE.

AND now this 22d day of August 1800, it is ordered by the Court, that the Petitioners be permitted to send the brigantine *Amelia*, in the petition mentioned, on a voyage from Philadelphia to St. Sebastians and back to Philadelphia, upon their entering into stipulation in the sum of six thousand dollars with approved security, as well for the safe return of the same vessel to Philadelphia, as for the payment to the said Respondent, his Heirs, Executors and Administrators, of one fourth of the freight of the same vessel for the said voyage out and home, deducting all reasonable and just mercantile charges.

ORDER

From a Magistrate for the Survey of a Vessel.

To A, B, C, D, &c.

You are hereby required to repair on board the brig *Mercurius*, now riding at anchor. in the Port of Baltimore, and examine the same brig whether she is too leaky or otherwise unfit in her crew, body, tackle, apparel, furniture, provisions or stores to proceed on her intended voyage to the Port of Oporto in Portugal. And make report to me in writing under your hands or the hands of any two of you, whether in any or in what respect the said brig is unfit to proceed on the aforesaid intended voyage, and what addition of men, provisions or stores, or what repairs or alterations in her body, tackle or apparel of the said brig will be necessary, agreeably the act of Congress of the United States in such cases made and provided.—Given under my Hand and Seal this first day June, seventeen hundred and ninety-seven.

(Seal.)

Commission of Appraisement and Sale.

GEORGE the Third, by the grace of God, of *Great Britain, France* and *Ireland*, king, defender of the faith : to ――― of ――― in the county of ――― gentleman, and ――― greeting. Whereas our beloved Sir *James Marriott*, knight and doctor of laws, our lieutenant of the high court of Admiralty of England, and in the same court official principal, and commissary general and special, and president and judge thereof, lawfully constituted in a certain cause of substraction of wages, civil and maritime, moved and prosecuted before him in our said court, on behalf of ――― late steward of the ship called the ―――

(whereof —— now is or lately was master), her tackle, apparel and furniture, rightly and duly proceeding on the day of the date hereof, at the petition of the proctor of the said —— exhibiting an attestation of —— of —— shipwright, and setting forth that he hath carefully examined the ship in question, and finds her in the following situation, to wit. ——————
hath decreed a commission to issue for the appraisement and sale of the said ship, and directed the produce-money arising from such sale to be brought into the registry of our aforesaid court, to abide the further order of this court, (justice so requiring): We do therefore by these presents authorise and empower you, jointly and severally, and do strictly charge and command you, that you fail not to reduce into writing a full, true and perfect inventory of the said ship —— her tackle, apparel and furniture, and that you choose one good and lawful person well experienced in such affairs, and swear him faithfully and justly to appraise the same according to their true values, and that you so appraise and value, or cause the same to be appraised and valued; and, the appraisement being taken, that you expose or cause the aforesaid ship, her tackle, apparel and furniture, to be exposed to publick sale, and that you sell or cause the same to be sold to the best bidder, and that you bring or cause to be brought the produce-money arising from such sale into the registry of our aforesaid court, on or before the —— day of —— next ensuing, to abide the further order of our said court; and that at the

same time you duly transmit the said appraisement subscribed by you and the said appraiser, together with the account of such sale, also subscribed by you, to our aforesaid judge of our said court, or his surrogate, together with these presents.

Given at London, in our aforesaid court, under the great seal thereof, the —— day of —— in the year of our Lord —— and of our reign the ——

Commission of Sale.

GEORGE the Third, by the grace of God, of *Great Britain, France* and *Ireland*, king, defender of the faith: to —— of —— in the county of —— gentleman, greeting. Whereas our beloved Sir *James Marriott*, knight and doctor of laws, our lieutenant of the high court of our Admiralty of England, and in the same court official principal and commissary general and special, and president and judge thereof, lawfully constituted in a certain cause of —— *civil and maritime*, moved and prosecuted before him, in our said court, on behalf of —— against the ship or vessel called the —— (whereof —— is now or lately was master), her tackle, apparel and furniture, rightly and duly proceeding on the day of the date hereof, at the petition of the proctor of the said —— decreed a commission to issue to sell the said ship —— her tackle, apparel and furniture, (justice so requiring). We do therefore by these presents authorize, empower and strictly charge and command you, that you expose or cause the aforesaid ship ——— her tackle, apparel and furniture, to be exposed to publick sale, and that you sell or cause the same to be sold to the best bidder ; and that you bring or cause to be brought the produce-money arising from such sale into the registry of our aforesaid court, on or before the ——— day of ——— next ensuing, to be there kept for the use of the persons who shall be entitled thereto ; and that at the same time you duly transmit the account of such sale, subscribed by you, to our aforesaid judge of our said court, or his surrogate, together with these presents.

Given at London, in our aforesaid court, under the great seal thereof, the ——— day of ——— in the year of our Lord ——— and of our reign the ———

Monition to deliver up Ship's Register, at the Petition of an owner of three fourths.

GEORGE the Third, by the grace of God of *Great Britain, France* and *Ireland,* king, defender of the faith: To all and singular our vice-admirals, justices of the peace, mayors, sheriffs, bailiffs, constables, and all other our officers, ministers and others, as well within liberties and franchises as without, greeting: Whereas our beloved Sir *James Marriott,* knight and doctor of laws, our lieutenant of the high court of our Admiralty of England, and in the same court official principal and commissary general and special, and president and judge thereof, lawfully constituted and appointed in a certain cause or business, *civil and maritime*, moved and prosecuted before him in our said court, on behalf of ——— owner of three-fourth parts of the ship called the ———. against the said ship, her tackle, apparel and furniture, and against ——— the master and ——— the owner of one fourth part of the said ship in special, and all others in general, rightly and duly proceeding on the day of the date hereof, by interlocutory decree, at the petition of the proctor of the said ——— and on motion of counsel decreed the possession of the said ship to be delivered to the said ——— owner of three fourth parts thereof, and having the majority of interest therein, or to his lawful attorney for his use; and at the further petition of the proctor of the said ——— alleging that the said ——— and ——— or one of them, are in possession of the register belonging to the said ship ——— decreed a motion to issue against them to deliver up the same to the said ——— or to his said attorney: we do therefore, by these presents, authorize and empower you jointly and severally, and do strictly charge and command you, that you omit not by reason of any liberty or franchise, but that you monish or cause to be admonished peremptorily and personally, the said ——— and ——— to deliver up to the register belonging to the said ship ——— unto the said ——— or to his lawful attorney, immediately after the execution of these presents, upon them the said ——— and ——— under pain of the law and the peril which will fall thereon: and that you duly certify us, or our aforesaid judge, or his surrogate, what you shall do in the premises, together with these presents.

Given at London, in our aforesaid court, under the great seal thereof, the —— day of —— in the year of our Lord —— and of the reign the ——

Decree of Attachment.

GEORGE the third, by the grace of God, of *Great Britain, France,* and *Ireland,* king, defender of the faith: to all and singular our vice-admirals, justices of the peace, mayors, sheriffs, bailiffs, marshals, constables, and to all other our officers, ministers and others, as well within liberties and franchises as without, greeting.— Whereas our beloved sir James Marriott, knight and doctor of laws, our lieutenant of the high court of admiralty of England, and in the same court official principal and commissary general and special, and president and judge thereof, lawfully constituted and appointed in a certain cause of —— *civil and maritime,* moved and prosecuted before him, in our said court, on behalf of —— late a mariner of the ship called the —— (whereof —— was master), against the said ship, and against —— owner thereof, intervening, rightly and duly proceeding, on the —— day of —— last, at the petition of the proctor of the said —— alleging that the said —— is the more legal person from whom the truth in this behalf may be better found out and enquired, than from his proctor exercising from him, decreed the said —— to be monished and cited to appear before us or our aforesaid judge, or his surrogate, in the common-hall of Doctors' Commons, situate in the parish of St. Benedict, near St. Paul's Wharf, London, on the —— session of —— term; to wit. the —— day of —— next ensuing, between the hours of —— and —— in the forenoon of the same day, to answer personally, by virtue of his corporal oath, to the positions or articles of a certain summary petition given in and admitted in the said cause on behalf of the said —— and further to do and receive as to justice shall appertain. And whereas a decree to the effect aforesaid issued accordingly; and whereas on the —— day of —— last, the proctor of the said —— returned the said decree, with a certificate thereon indorsed, that the same had been duly executed, on the —— day of —— by showing the same under seal to —— notary publick, proctor for the said —— and by leaving with him a copy thereof; and whereas on the day of the date hereof, our aforesaid judge, at the petition of the proctor of the said —— decreed the aforesaid —— to be attached for his contempt, in not giving in his answers to the said summary petition, pursuant to the said decree, (justice so requiring): We do therefore strictly charge and command you, jointly and severally, that you omit not by reason of any liberty or franchise, but that you attach and arrest or cause to be attached and arrested the said —— and him so attached and arrested you keep under safe and secure arrest, until he shall have given his personal answers on oath to the positions or articles of the aforesaid summary petition, given in and admitted in the said cause, on the said —— aforesaid decree.

Given at London, in our aforesaid court, under the great seal thereof, the —— day of —— in the year of our Lord —— and of our reign the ——

Juratory Caution.

On —— day of —— before the worshipful —— doctor of laws and surrogate, in his chambers in Doctors' Commons, London; present, —— notary publick.

(Ship's name.)

Which day appeared personally —— of —— mariner, one of the parties in this cause, who submitting himself to the jurisdiction of this court, bound himself, his heirs, executors and administrators, in the sum of —— pounds of lawful money of Great Britain, unto —— master of the ship or vessel called the —— to prosecute the action commenced in this behalf, and to pay expences, in case he shall fail in this his suit, and to appear on —— the —— day of —— and so often afterwards as he shall be ordered by the judge or his surrogate; and unless he shall so do, he doth hereby consent that execution shall issue forth against him, his heirs, executors and administrators, goods and chattels wheresoever they shall be found, to the value of the sum above-mentioned; and the said —— made oath, that he would appear on —— the —— day of —— and so often afterwards as he shall be ordered by the judge or his surrogate.

Decree of Possession.

GEORGE the Third, by the grace of God, of *Great Britain, France* and *Ireland,* king, defender of the faith: to —— gentleman, marshal of the high court of our admiralty of England, and to his deputy whomsoever, greeting. Whereas our beloved the right worshipful Sir *James Marriott,* knight and doctor of laws, our lieutenant of the said high court of Admiralty of England, and in the same court official principal and commissary general and special, and president and judge thereof, lawfully constituted and appointed, in a certain cause or business, *civil and maritime,* moved and prosecuted before him, in our said court, on behalf of —— owner of —— parts of the ship called the —— against the said ship, her tackle, apparel and furniture, and against —— the master, and —— the owner of —— part of the said ship, in special, and all others in general, rightly and duly proceeding on the day of the date hereof, his interlocutory decree, at the petition of the proctor of the said —— and on motion of counsel, decreed the possession of the said ship to the —— to be delivered to the said —— owner of ——

parts thereof, and having the majority of interest therein, or to his lawful attorney for his use; and at the further petition of the proctor of the said —— alleging that the said —— and —— or one of them, are in possession of the register belonging to the said ship the —— decreed a monition to issue against them, to deliver up the same unto the said —— (justice so requiring) : We do therefore by these presents authorize and empower you, jointly and severally, and do strictly charge and command you, to release the said ship the —— her tackle, apparel and furniture, from the arrest made in this behalf, and to deliver the possession thereof to the said —— owner of —— parts thereof, and having the majority of interest therein, or to his lawful attorney, for his use: and hereof fail not.

Given at London, in our aforesaid court, under the great seal thereof, the —— day of —— in the year of our Lord —— and of our reign the ——

Restitution.

GEORGE the Third, by the grace of God, of *Great Britain, France* and *Ireland*, king, defender of the faith : to all persons in whose custody or possession the undermentioned —— or any part or parcel thereof be and remain, greeting : Whereas our beloved Sir *James Marriott*, knight and doctor of laws, our lieutenant of the high court of our Admiralty of England, and in the same court official principal and commissary general and special, and president and judge thereof, lawfully constituted, in a certain business moved and prosecuted before him, in our said court, on our behalf, in our office of Admiralty, against —— found floating upon the high seas and brought to the port of —— and against ———— claimant of the said —— intervening, rightly and duly proceeding on the day of the date hereof, by his interlocutory decree, by consent of our procurator general, in our office of Admiralty, and also of the proctor of the salvors (who alleged that his parties had received the sum of —— in full of all salvage and other demands) pronounced the said —— to belong as claimed, and decreed the same to be restored to the said claimant, for the use of the owners and proprietors thereof (justice so requiring): We therefore by these presents authorize and empower you, jointly and severally, and do strictly charge and command you to release the said —— from the arrest made in his behalf and to deliver and restore the same unto the said —— the claimant, for the use of the owners and proprietors thereof: and hereof fail not at your peril.

Given at London, in our aforesaid court, under the great seal thereof, the —— day of —— in the year of our Lord —— and of our reign the ——

Libel for Assault and Battery.*

TO THE HONOURABLE JAMES WINCHESTER, &c.

The Libel of George Fortune humbly showeth:

That your Libellant on the —— of ——— in the year —— at the port of Baltimore, shipped as a mariner on board the ship Serpent, whereof John Wheeler was master, to perform a voyage on the high seas and within the jurisdiction of this Honourable Court, to wit, from Baltimore to Martinique and thence back to the said port of Baltimore:

That during the said voyage to Martinique on the —— day of ——— in the year aforesaid, while your Libellant, in obedience to the orders of the said master, was arranging some planks in the steerage to form a bed for a sick passenger, your Libellant was assaulted by the said J. W. who jumped from the deck down on the head and shoulders of your Libellant; struck your Libellant in the mouth with his fist, and most cruelly and inhumanely beat your Libellant over the head with a doubled rope to the ends of

---

* As I understand that in some of the District Courts of the United States, suits for assault and battery, though committed on the high seas, are not held to be within their jurisdiction, it is proper to add, that libels for such offences were never dismissed, on that ground, by the late Judge Winchester, whose opinion is entitled to the highest respect. He required that the assault and battery should be stated with every degree of minuteness as to the time, place and manner. The respondent was bound to be equally particular in the defence which he might make.

which were fastened a pair of sharp iron can hooks with which he cut your Libellant on the head severely in several places, so that your Libellant bled profusely; and the said J. W. also, at the same time, struck your Libellant on the head with a large billet of wood, which he afterwards threw at your Libellant.

Your Libellant further showeth, that while the said ship lay at Martinique, to wit, on the ―――― day of ―――― aforesaid, because he requested the said J. W. to hire and employ two seamen to assist in navigating the ship in the place of two who had run away, was assaulted and severely beaten by the said J. W. with a rope, and afterwards forcibly taken from the vessel to the town of St. Pierre, where your Libellant was imprisoned and there detained in prison, for the space of twenty four hours until the next day, when the ship was ready to sail.

To the end, therefore, that your Libellant may obtain satisfaction in damages for the injuries by him sustained in the premises, he prays process of attachment against the said J. W. that he may answer to this Libel upon oath, and the following

Interrogatories:

1st. Did you assault and beat the Libellant at the several times and in the manner stated in the Libel? If yea, what was the cause?

2. Did you strike the Libellant with the can hooks? If yea, how often did you strike him?

And your Libellant prays that by Decree of this Honourable Court, the said J. W. may be compelled to pay your Libellant such sum of money for damages as to your honour may seem just. And he will pray, &c.

WILLIAM GWYNN,
Proc. pro Lib.

29th May, 1808.

Answer to a Libel for Assault and Battery.

TO THE HONOURABLE JAMES WINCHESTER, &C.

The answer and defence of William Core, mate of the ship Becky, to the Libel of William Hampton.

This Respondent saving and reserving all manner of benefit of exceptions to the said Libel and the many untruths therein contained for answer thereto, saith,

That the Libellant did ship as a mariner on board the Becky to perform the voyage stated in his Libel; but this Respondent denies that the Libellant during all the said voyage performed his duty as a faithful and obedient mariner; for this Respondent says, that at the time complained of, in the said Libel, there being then a heavy gale and high sea, this Respondent, as his duty and the safety of the vessel required, directed the Libellant, who was then aloft, to shift the foresail, and this Respondent handed the Libellant an earring, or small rope, for the purpose of tying the said sail; that the Libellant refused to do as he was directed, on pretence that the rope was too short: and when this

Respondent, urged by the danger in which the vessel then was, for want of a sail to keep her to the wind, insisted that the Libellant should make the attempt to fasten the sail, the Libellant replied, " I wont pass it—I'll be d—d if I do for you or any body else :" That this Respondent then went to the Libellant and struck him once with his open hand on the side of the head, and again ordered him to pass the earring : that the Libellant still refused and attempted to strike this Respondent, and continued to resist and refuse to perform his duty, until this Respondent struck him twice with his fist; and then the Libellant fastened the sail with the same earring which he, at first, said was too short.

This Respondent further says that he did not beat the Libellant at any time during the said voyage, in any other manner than is above stated; and this Respondent denies that the life of the Libellant was in any manner endangered by the beating or correction above stated, or that he was thereby prevented from doing his duty or otherwise damaged as stated in the aforesaid Libel. And this Respondent says that his duty as an officer and the safety of the vessel made it necessary for him to correct the Libellant as before stated.

Wherefore this Respondent prays that he may be considered as justified in the premises and be hence dismissed with costs. And he will pray, &c.

WILLIAM GWYNN,
Proc. pro Res.

18*th May,* 1801.

BALTIMORE COUNTY, ss.

On this ——day of —— 1801, before me, a Justice of the Peace for the County aforesaid, came the above Respondent, W. C. and made oath, that the facts as stated in the above answer are true.

O. D.

FINIS.

TABLE OF CONTENTS.

Advertisement,   III

PART I.

Historical Essay on the Civil Jurisdiction of the Admiralty,   VII
Ordinance of Hastings on the subject of Admiralty Jurisdiction,   XIX
Heads of the Articles of Inquisition taken at Quinborow in the year 1376. in the 49th of Edward III. by eighteen expert seamen. before William Nevil. Admiral of the North, Philip Courteney. Admiral of the West, and the Lord Latimer, Warden of the Cinque Ports,   XIX
The complaint of the Lord Admiral of England concerning prohibitions from the Common Law Courts,   XXII
Lord Coke's Answer to this complaint,   XXIII
Resolution upon the cases of Admiral Jurisdiction,   XXIV
The Jurisdiction of Admiralty settled,   XXVI

PART II.

Preface,
Tit. 1. Of the manner of instituting or commencing an action in the High Court of Admiralty of England; and of the form of the original warrant, or mandate which is to be impetrated in maritime causes,   3
    Citation, what it is,   5
Tit. 2. Of the direction of the warrant,   9
Tit. 3. Of the manner of executing the warrant,   10
Tit. 4. Of the caution or bail to be given by the person who is arrested, for his legal appearance,   11
    Of the different kinds of bail,   12
Tit. 5. What shall constitute a legal appearance,   13
Tit. 6. The execution of the warrant,   14
Tit. 7. Of the warrant of Attorney or Proxy, what it is,   14
Tit. 8. Of constituting a Proctor *apud acta*, or extrajudicially before a Notary,   17
    How and when Proctors may be used,   19

CONTENTS.

Tit. 8. When a Proctor is said to cease to be a Proctor in a cause, and when not,   20

Tit. 9. The petition of the Plaintiff's Proctor at the time of the return of the warrant before the Judge,   24

Tit. 10. The petition of the Defendant upon perfecting his legal appearance, according to the stipulation, and the Plaintiff not appearing or neglecting to prosecute his suit,   26

Tit. 11. The petition of the Proctors *hinc inde*, if both parties appear,   28

Tit. 12. Of the fidejussory security given by the Defendant, and the stipulation which is entered into by him,   29

Tit. 13. The petition and protest of the Proctor for the Plaintiff at the introduction of fidejussores of this kind,   30

Tit. 14. The production of fidejussores on the part of the Plaintiff,   30

Tit. 15. The petition of the Proctor for better or more substantial security,   31

Tit. 16. The decree of the Judge on the petition for further security,   33

Tit. 17. The manner of proving the sufficiency or insufficiency of the fidejussores,   33

Tit. 18. The security to be interposed by the principal party to indemnify his fidejussores,   34

Tit. 19. The giving or tendering a Libel,   34
    Term probatory, what it is,   36
    Proof, of the different kinds of,   ib.
    Commission sub mutuæ vicissitudinis, or Letters Rogatory, and Commissions of Dedimus Potestatem,   37

Tit. 20. The manner of certifying the decree to answer the allegations of the Libel, if the Defendant cannot be cited,   43

Tit. 21. The manner of executing the aforesaid arrants *viis et modis*,   44

Tit. 22. The Petition of the Proctor for the Plaintiff, when the fidejussores on the part of the defendant being monished to bring in the principal, neither appear themselves nor have him forthcoming,   45

Tit. 23. The petition of the fidejussores if they appear on the day appointed for them to bring in the principal party,   48

Tit. 24. The production of the principal party, and the punishment to be inflicted upon him if he refuse to submit to an examination under oath,   50

CONTENTS.

Tit. 25. The requisition and production of Witnesses, and the manner of proceeding if they refuse to be examined,	52
Tit. 26. Compulsory process against Witnesses who are summoned and do not appear,	53
Tit. 27. The petitition for and issuing of a Commission for the examination of Witnesses residing at a distance from the place where the Court sits,	54
Of Commissions,	55
Tit. 28. Of the warrant to be impetrated *in rem* where the Debtor absconds, or is absent from the Realm,	60
Of Attachments,	ib.
Tit. 29. Of the execution of the aforesaid warrant,	68
Tit. 30. Certificate of the execution of the warrant for the attachment of the goods,	ib.
Tit. 31. The exhibition or return of the said warrant and the petition of the Proctor for the Plaintiff,	69
Tit. 32. The manner of attaching goods or debts in the hands of others, to which the officer cannot have access.	70
Tit. 33. The certificate of the aforesaid warrant against goods remaining in the possession of another,	71
Tit. 34. Of the manner of proceeding on the appearance of the person in whose hands the goods were attached,	id.
Tit. 35. The granting of the second, third and fourth default,	73
Tit. 36. What things are contained in the aforesaid article upon the first decree,	76
Tit. 37. Of the manner of proceeding if the person appear to whom the goods which have been attached belongs,	77
Tit. 38. Of the appearance of a third person to claim goods which have been attached as the property of another,	78
Tit. 39. Of a third person intervening for his interest after the first decree,	79
Tit. 40. That the Plaintiff may obtain a first decree as well against the person to whom the goods which are attached are alleged to belong, as against all others who do not appear,	80
Tit. 41. The manner of arresting your own goods when they are detained, occupied or possessed by another,	81
Jurisdiction of the Court *in personam*, and of the Prize Jurisdiction,	82
Tit. 42. The manner of proceeding in possessory and petitory actions,	84
Tit. 43. Sequestration of the goods *pendente lite*,	88
Tit. 44. The arrest of goods by different creditors,	89

CONTENTS.

Tit. 45. Of the oath of calumny and what clauses are contained in it.	ib.
Tit. 46. The proposing matter of defence, of propounding exceptions and of corroborating the evidence of witnesses,	92
Tit. 47. The suppletory oath,	93
Tit. 48. The exhibition of instruments in support of the allegations of the parties,	95
Tit. 49. The Comparison of Letters,	86
Tit. 50. The exhibition of instruments of writing in the French, Italian or German Language in support of the Libel or other matter proposed,	ib.
Tit. 51. The exhibition of the translation together with the original, and the petition of the Proctor who presents it,	98
Of the different kinds of instruments,	98
Tit. 52. The conclusion of the cause and the manner of giving information to the Judge before pronouncing the sentence and the manner of pronouncing the same,	99
Tit. 53. Of an appeal from the definitive sentence,	ib.
Of appeal from writs of error in the U. States, 100	106
Tit. 54. That it is not lawful to appeal from grievances, or an interlocutory decree not having the effect of a definitive sentence,	102
Tit. 55. What shall be called an irreparable grievance and a decree waiving the effect of a definitive sentence, from which it is lawful to appeal,	ib.
Tit. 56. Appeal from the Court of Admiralty,	104
Whether an appeal from any interlocutory decree may be allowed from a District to a Circuit Court?	105
Tit. 57. Of the Inhibition of the Appeal,	106
Writs of Inhibition in the United States,	107
Tit. 58. Form of the execution or certificate of the aforesaid Inhibition,	107
Tit. 59. Of putting in fidejussory security in the Appeal,	108
Tit. 60. The manner of proceeding in a case of appeal,	110
Tit. 61. Of the petition for a decree to show cause why sentence of execution ought not to be demanded.	ib.
Tit. 62. Of the sentence of execution,	111
Tit. 63. The decree against the principal party to pay the sum adjudged with costs,	112
Tit. 64. Decree or monition against the fidejussores to pay the thing adjudged, if the principal party abscond,	ib.
Tit. 65. The decree against the fidejussores to pay the sum adjudged, without regard to the decree against the principal party.	113

CONTENTS.

Tit. 66. Peremption of suit, 114
Tit. 67. The manner of proceeding in causes of contempt, 115
Tit. 68. The appearance of the person who is attached in a case of contempt, 116

PART III.

A brief Discourse, showing the order or structure of a Libel or Declaration, 129
Summons from a Judge or Justice of the Peace to the Master, to answer a claim for wages, 128
Certificate of the Magistrate to the Clerk of the District Court, 129
Libel for Seamen's wages, 130
Attachment against the vessel, or person, 132
Monition against the vessel, or person, 133
Libel for materials furnished to a vessel, 135
Libel in a case of damage, 136
Libel for salvage in a case of wreck, 140
———————— in a case of recapture, 144, 154
Answers to the above Libels, 146, 157
Libel for the restitution of a vessel captured without authority, 149
Plea to Jurisdiction, 151
Replication to a Plea to Jurisdiction, 153
Protest to evidence, 164
Libel on a Bottomry Bond, 167
Libel in a case of Hypothecation, 169
Replication, 174
Rejoinder, 179
Forfeiture of a ship on account of her being falsely registered, 184
Claim and Answer, 186
Libel for the recovery of property illegally captured, 189
Claim, 191
Recusant Owners, 192
Replication, 193
Decree, 195
Order from a Magistrate for the survey of a vessel, ib.
Commission of appraisement and sale, 196
Commission of sale, 198
Monition to deliver up a ship's register at the petition of an owner of three-fourths, 199
Decree of Attachment, 201
Juratory Caution, 203
Decree of Possession, 204
Restitution, 205
Libel for Assault and Battery, 207
Answer, 209